Transits

Reinhold Ebertin

First Printing 1928
Current Printing 1995
ISBN: 0-86690-094-2

Cover design by Phil Riske
Translation by Linda Kratzsch

Published by:
American Federation of Astrologers, Inc.
PO Box 22040
6535 S. Rural Road
Tempe, AZ 85285-2040

Printed in the United States of America

Contents

Preface

In the preface to the first edition in 1928 it was pointed out that the transits, i.e. the passage of the progressing stellar bodies over the interpretive factors of the basic horoscope, provide the best and most easily understood introduction to astrology or cosmobiology. Those who have comprehended this method of work can also quickly master the more difficult sectors of astrological research into character and fate. The examples given in this book have been taken from real life and show to what extent prognostications based on the transits do indeed agree with fact.

At the time of publication of this book in 1928, documentation on Neptune was still new, hardly being included in other textbooks. Now the effects of Pluto are to be added. Although only twenty years' knowledge has been gained on this planet, so much material is available that a well-founded documentation on this "outsider" among the stellar bodies can be presented.

To differentiate between the positive and negative inclinations, the signs + and - have been chosen; the conjunctions have been designated by (C), as it is not always possible to derive the favorable or unfavorable trends form the aspects alone.

This book of transits has become the steady companion of many thousands of people. Many readers have had to acquire a second or even third copy because the pages of the first not only were too worn from frequent reading, but had been literally read to pieces. I trust and hope that this new, completely revised edition will gain just as many true friends.

Reinhold Ebertin
Aalen/Wuertt, 1952

The 1971 edition remained, for the most part, unrevised, but was supplemented. Please note the Appendix.

The Ebertin Method: A World-Wide Success

Forty years ago Ebertin undertook a comparison of the various methods and looked for the elements of conformity. In his journal "Kosmobiologie" he then formulated problems of research (up to now, these number more than seventy) to find the best way of finding the best solutions.

It was proven that the following elements can be considered fundamental: The zodiac of twelve signs is divided into 360 degrees and applied primarily as a measuring circle; the positions of the stellar bodies and their aspects, including the half-sums. Much of the medieval "accessoires" can be dispensed with. The orb of the aspects must be greatly reduced in order to achieve better results with fewer but more certain elements.

The ninety degree circle represents a great alleviation, making it possible to grasp all the interrelations with greater ease. A better comparison of cosmograms is warranted by uniform forms where the point of Cancer is always at the top.

The structural pictures, graphic representations, and the cosmo-psychograms, the contact-cosmograms, the annual curves, etc. are extremely convincing in their illustrative quality.

This method has most particularly made its friends in scientific circles. Ebertin speaks of cosmobiology in contrast to astrology. This contrast is most readily seen in the elimination of the questionable houses which are supposed to correspond to the individual facets of life, but which are frequently misleading; and in the consideration of not only the cosmic factor, but also of the influences of heredity, environment, milieu, occupation, etc., and thereby ruling out any fatalistic tendency.

Those who wish to delve into this method further can refer to *Mensch im All*, an introduction to calculation, elaboration and evaluation; *The Combination of Stellar Influences*, the internationally acknowledged work on interpretation; *Applied Cosmobiology*, a comprehensive textbook presenting an introduction into the use of the ninety degree workboard and serving as a guide for investigations in all areas of life.

The Ebertin method has in the past years spread its influence throughout the world. Contributing to this expansion has been the international Congresses for Cosmobiological Research, held since 1949, the many articles published here and abroad by the author and on the author, the Ebertin study associations in Australia and North America, the lectures at congresses in Europe and America, and the translations of many of the books on this method.

1

The Cosmogram

The term cosmogram designates the notation of a cosmic constellation. The word "horoscope" has been avoided in this book; the popularization of astrology through newspapers and magazines has changed the meaning of this word completely. Originally, it meant "hourly view," i.e. the heavenly constellations as observed and recorded for a particular hour. In the press, horoscope is given to mean a statement based on the position of the Sun in the various signs of the zodiac without regard to the hour of birth or correlation to the other stellar bodies.

The use of the term "stellar bodies" in this book is deliberate, so as to include Sun, Moon, and the planets as well. The Sun and Moon are not planets and therefore cannot be so designated, as is, unfortunately, often the case in many books on astrology.

The foundation for casting the cosmogram is the zodiac, which the Sun moves through in one year (Illustration 1).

It is advisable to memorize the signs of the zodiac using this illustration, if they have not already been learned from the calendars. Each of these signs supplies the name for thirty smaller divisions which we call degrees. Accordingly, the whole circle contains 360 degrees (Illustration 2).

To locate the positions of the stellar bodies in the zodiac more exactly, one degree is divided into sixty minutes and every minute is again divided into sixty seconds. This subdivision is so fine that it cannot be portrayed in a zodiacal chart. Therefore, the position of each stellar

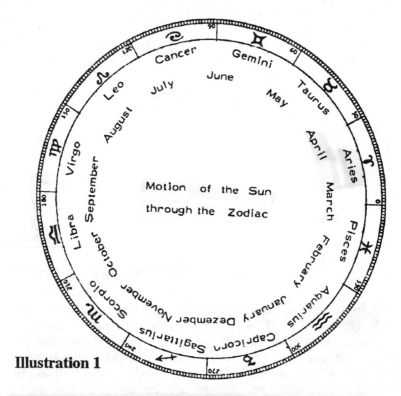

Illustration 1

body is written in degrees, minutes, and, sometimes, in seconds. When talking of minutes and seconds as designations of a star's position we do not mean minutes and seconds in terms of space. For this reason, when talking of time, we use the symbols "h" for hour, "m" for minute, and "s" for second.

In addition to the stellar bodies, we compute in reference to time that point of the zodiac which is highest at the time of birth, i.e. culminates (Midheaven or medium coeli) and that point of the zodiac which is just rising in the east—the point of ascent or Ascendant. Drawing

One sign equals 30 degrees

Illustration 2

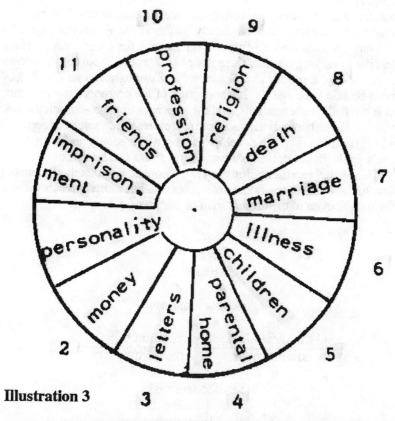

Illustration 3

a straight line from the Ascendant through the center of the zodiac, we can consider the upper half to represent the visible part and the lower half the invisible part of the firmament. If a straight line is drawn from Midheaven through the center of the zodiacal circle, the left hand side is that part of the sky where the stars are on the Ascendant, and the right hand side is where those stars are recorded which have crossed the Midheaven and descend opposite the Ascendant.

The space within the zodiac is usually divided into twelve sectors or houses, the first of which begins at the Ascendant, as Illustration 3 shows.

These sectors or houses are supposed to represent certain facets of life. The first house is said to characterize the personality of an individual, the second house refers to money matters, the third house shows relations to brothers and sisters and to neighbors, and also to correspondence, etc. The meaning of each section can be seen in Illustration 3.

These days, we are all accustomed to a critical view of traditional

3

science, and this division into houses after the manner of a fortune teller is no longer acceptable, and not only that, there are also various systems of house division, none of which agrees with the other, thus perforce leading to varying results. The author has thoroughly covered this topic in his book *Charakter and Schicksal in Kosmogramm* so that it only need be said here that the lower portion of the cosmogram represents, as it were, the subconscious, and the upper portion ego-consciousness; and the Ascendant or horizontal line represents the sphere of experience where the individual can develop his inborn potentiality and achieve his life's goals. In short, the following equivalents can be given:

This spatial representation does not renounce completely its connection to the old form of house interpretation, but rather, presents it in a form clear even to the critical man of our present day.

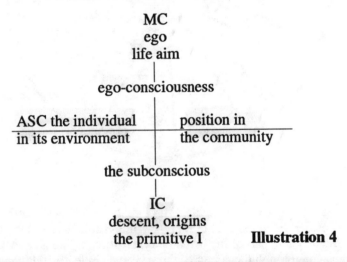

MC
ego
life aim

ego-consciousness

ASC the individual   position in
in its environment   the community

the subconscious

IC
descent, origins
the primitive I   **Illustration 4**

If, for example, there are many stellar bodies present in the lower half of the cosmogram, the subconscious forces of an individual will tend to be strong; however, there will be difficulties encountered in achieving goals in actual life, because the consciousness of self is, as opposed to the unconscious forces, not potent enough. The upper half of the cosmogram being occupied to a great extent means that this particular individual takes his fate into his own hands and attempts to realize all his plans with great expenditure of energy. If there are many stars at the Ascendant, then such persons are well able to assert themselves; stars gathered at the Descendant indicate the more important role played by communal life (marriage, teamwork, public life).

Prerequisite to setting up a prognostication for the future is a close examination of the cosmogram itself. It is clear that only those disposi-

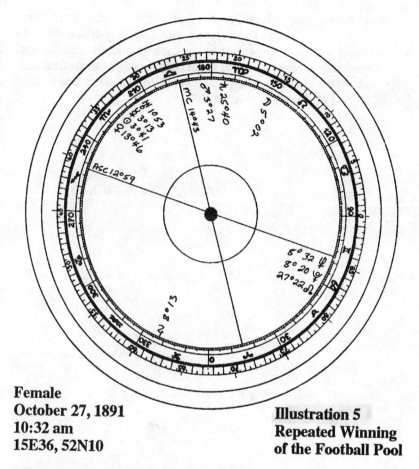

Female
October 27, 1891
10:32 am
15E36, 52N10

Illustration 5
Repeated Winning
of the Football Pool

tions, talents and potential already inherent can be developed and realized.

The cosmogram, which is set up for the moment of birth, is also called the basic horoscope, root or radical horoscope.

Illustration 5 shows the cosmogram of a woman born on October 27, 1891, who, in the years from 1950 to 1952, won the football pool several times.

This case has already been treated by Georg Hoffmann in the journal "Kosmobiologie," so that no one can claim that the author has only invented this example.

In the drawing, the Ascendant is on the left at 12 Sagittarius 59 and the Midheaven is situated at 14 Libra 43. These two locations are called the personal points of the cosmogram because, in conjunction with the stellar positions, these points can hardly be held in common with other persons, as they are related to the place of birth and calculated according to the exact time of birth. These points move by approximately one degree within just four minutes of time. The individual stellar bodies can with some deviation be shared by those born on the same day, but place and time result in a varying relationship of the stars to the Ascendant and Midheaven.

2

Aspects in the Cosmogram

The significance of the constellations is derived from the positions in each sign of the zodiac, from the relation to the Ascendant and Midheaven, possibly also from the system of houses, and, too, from the angular relationship of one to another. Indeed, the observation has often been made that these angles or aspects are of greater significance than the positions in sign or house. An angle is formed when straight lines are drawn from one point in different directions (rays).

In the cosmogram, an angle is formed by a connection of the center point with two different points in the zodiac. But not just any aspect is suitable for our calculations. A system of angles is produced by a manifold division through the center point so that two stars can be at the same point of the zodiac, as in Illustration 5, for example, Sun and Mercury in the sign Scorpio in a conjunction; the stars can be opposite one another on the bisecting line of the circle, as here Moon and Jupiter, which is then called opposition, or an aspect of 180 degrees. If the halves of the circle are themselves bisected, we get quarter circles, designated square with a distance of ninety degrees. Here, Moon and Neptune or Pluto are square. And then comes the semisquare meaning forty-five degrees. Saturn and Venus are semisquare.

Another system of aspects results from a division by three of the circle. The circle has 360 degrees. This is a trine, here between Jupiter and the Sun or Venus. A half-trine is one-sixth of the circle or a sextile, meaning sixty degrees to be found here between Sun and Moon.

The aspects may be very accurate, in which case these are termed

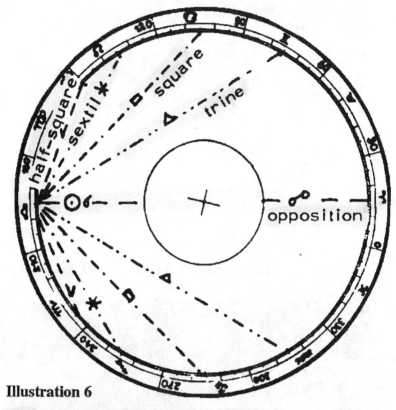

Illustration 6

exact. The square between Jupiter and Neptune is precisely ninety degrees with a very slight deviation in the minutes. If the orb, i.e. the radius, is greater, then the aspect is termed platic, not exact, for example, as between Jupiter and Uranus, where the difference amounts to approximately seven degrees. In traditional astrology, a very wide orb or radius was used in calculation, sometimes up to fifteen degrees on each side. There may be some cases where this is justified. Nowadays a radius of five degrees to either side should not be exceeded. Illustration 6 gives a comprehensive survey of the aspects from one point.

If a stellar body is at fifteen degrees Libra, as is the Sun here, there should correspondingly be a star situated at the same place within a few degrees radius in the case of conjunction. An opposition is then at fifteen degrees Aries, the squares at fifteen degrees Cancer and Capricorn, semisquare at zero degrees Virgo and Sagittarius, the trines at fifteen degrees Gemini and Aquarius, and the sextiles at fifteen degrees Leo and Sagittarius.

3

What Is A Transit?

The word transit means so much as a going over, and in our sense, a planet's passage over another. The stellar bodies in the cosmogram are considered primarily to be called the radix, with each of the radical stars marked by "r." Accordingly, Sun r 3° Scorpio means that the Sun is to be found in the radix, in the natal cosmogram. The stars in motion are designated "progressing," abbreviated "p." If, then, Uranus p is at fourteen degrees Cancer, it is in relation to the Midheaven (M) in our example at fourteen degrees Libra. Then we speak of Uranus p square M r. A transit means then the aspect of a progressing stellar body to a stellar body in the radix.

Contrary to the transits, we also use directions for calculation, whereby the stars in the radix are directed according to a particular key and themselves form aspects. For this reason, it is absolutely and always necessary to add the symbols r and p in the notations.

Now we come to the problem of when the stars in progression come into relation with the signification points of the radical chart. In order to obtain a quick overall view, it is advisable to choose a zodiacal chart with two graduated circles, so that in the outer ring the aspects to the various stellar bodies as well as to the Ascendant and Midheaven can be entered. If the position of a stellar body in progression is known, the aspects can be immediately read.

Illustration 7 shows the cosmogram with the points of aspect. We start, for example, with Sun and Mercury, which here are both at three degrees Scorpio. Across from this point is the opposition at three

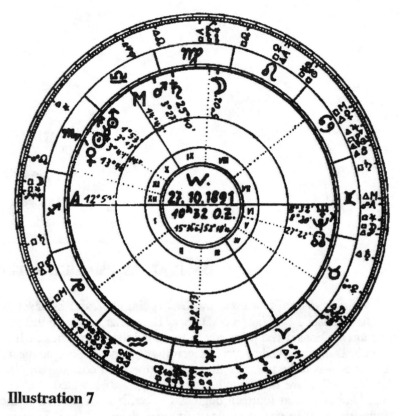

Illustration 7

degrees Taurus; we note thus ☍☉☿. The points of the square are at three degrees Leo and Aquarius, and we write the symbols □☉☿. At three degrees Cancer and Pisces we find the points of trine—△☉☿. The conjunctions do not have to be noted because the stellar points are sufficiently prominent in the cosmogram. We have excluded the sextiles in the illustration. Aside from that, the effect of the sextiles is here negligible. The semisquares and sesquiquadrates have also not been marked.

Once the cosmogram has so far been set up, it is very easy to read the aspects of the stellar bodies in progression to the radical stars. Which brings us to the question of where the daily constellations can be found. For ages, man has observed the heavens and has also recorded the individual stellar progressions. Nowadays, we know the constellations for years in advance, exactly computed and contained in the astronomical ephemerides.

10

4

How to read the Ephemeris

About 120 years ago, the astronomer Harding in Göttingen published the German ephemerides, but which were discontinued soon after. The publication of the *Raphael Ephemerides* was commenced in 1830 in London, and these gradually took the fore internationally. Only in 1917 did a German publishing house begin to issue another annual ephemeris. After the Second World War, Ebertin-Verlag in Aalen took the initiative and brought out a pocket ephemeris, each new annual publication revised and improved, and which has become more widely used from year to year.

Illustration 8 shows the two pages for February 1952. Under the days of the month, Sunday has been underlined to facilitate reading the days of the week. The column for sidereal time is of no account for the observation of transits; it is necessary for determining the Ascendant and Midheaven for a particular time of the day. In the Sun column we find Longitude and Dec. = Declination. Longitude means the graduation of the zodiac. Declination is the deviation of the solar orbit from the celestial equator. Of primary interest for us is the solar longitude. For instance, on February 1 the Sun is at 14°34'50'$\approx$ = Aquarius. The entries in this ephemeris are made for midday 12 o'clock, Greenwich Mean time, which corresponds to 1 p.m. Central European Time. Many ephemerides go by midnight 12 a.m. Greenwich Mean Time, but for transit observations the midday ephemerides are always preferable, because the diurnal constellations are our subject of interest. The midday ephemerides also have an advantage for other computations. As

Februar 1962 February

Tag Day	Sternzeit Sidereal Time h m s	Sonne - Sun: Länge - Long.	Sonne - Sun: Dekl. - Dec.	Mond - Moon: Länge - Long. 12h	Mond - Moon: Länge - Long. 0h	Mond - Moon: Breite - Lat.	Mond - Moon: Dekl. - Dec.	Mond - Moon: Knoten - Node
1	20 42 36	11°♒34'50"	17°S19	25°♈43'	2°♉15'	4°N19	13°N58	1°♓47'
2	20 46 32	12 35 44	17 02	8♉41	15 02	4 53	19 01	1 44
3	20 50 29	13 36 37	16 45	21 18	27 29	5 12	23 06	1 41
4	20 54 25	14 37 28	16 27	3♊37	9♊41	5 16	26 03	1 38
5	20 58 22	15 38 17	16 09	15 43	21 42	5 05	27 44	1 35
6	21 02 18	16 39 05	15 51	27 39	3♋36	4 42	28 07	1 31
7	21 06 15	17 39 52	15 33	9♋31	15 25	4 06	27 12	1 28
8	21 10 12	18 40 38	15 14	21 20	27 14	3 21	25 03	1 25
9	21 14 08	19 41 22	14 55	3♌09	9♌05	2 26	21 50	1 22
10	21 18 05	20 42 07	14 36	15 02	21 00	1 25	17 41	1 19
11	21 22 01	21 42 46	14 16	26 59	3♍00	0 20	12 50	1 16
12	21 25 58	22 43 26	13 57	9♍03	15 08	0 S 47	7 27	1 12
13	21 29 54	23 44 05	13 37	21 15	27 25	1 53	1 45	1 09
14	21 33 51	24 44 42	13 17	3♎38	9♎54	2 54	4 S 06	1 06
15	21 37 47	25 45 18	12 56	16 13	22 36	3 47	9 53	1 03
16	21 41 44	26 45 53	12 35	29 03	5♏35	4 31	15 22	1 00
17	21 45 40	27 46 27	12 15	12♏11	18 51	5 02	20 16	0 56
18	21 49 37	28 46 59	11 54	25 37	2♐28	5 17	24 17	0 53
19	21 53 34	29 47 30	11 33	9♐24	16 25	5 14	27 02	0 50
20	21 57 30	0♓48 00	11 12	23 31	0♑43	4 53	28 10	0 47
21	22 01 27	1 48 29	10 50	7♑58	15 18	4 13	27 25	0 44
22	22 05 23	2 48 57	10 28	22 41	0♒07	3 15	24 45	0 41
23	22 09 20	3 49 22	10 07	7♒35	15 04	2 04	20 23	0 37
24	22 13 16	4 49 47	9 45	22 32	29 59	0 45	14 43	0 34
25	22 17 13	5 50 10	9 22	7♓25	14♓46	0 N 38	8 12	0 31
26	22 21 10	6 50 31	9 00	22 04	29 17	1 57	1 22	0 28
27	22 25 06	7 50 50	8 38	6♈25	13♈27	3 06	5 N 24	0 25
28	22 29 03	8 51 08	8 15	20 22	27 11	4 03	11 42	0 22
29	22 32 59	9 51 23	7 53	3♉53	10♉29	4 44	17 16	0 18

Gegenseitige Aspekte / Mutual Aspects

Tag	Aspekt
1	♀ ✱ ♂
2	♃ □ ♅
4	☉ △ ♄
5	♀ ☌ ♅
	♀ □ ♃
8	♀ □ ♄
10	☿ ✱ ♅
	☉ ☍ ♇
11	☉ △ ♆
12	☿ △ ♄
14	♂ △ ♅
	♀ □ ♆
15	☿ ☍ ♇
16	☿ △ ♆
21	♅ ☍ ♄
22	☉ ☌ ☿
26	☿ △ ♅
28	☿ △ ♂
29	☉ △ ♅

Mondaspekte - Lunar Aspects

Tag	☉	♇	♆	♅	♄	♃	♂	♀	☿
1		△	☍						□
2	☽ 20h01			✱			☍	△	
3		□							
4									△
5	△	✱	△		△	✱			
6									
7				☌	□	□	△	☍	
8	F		□						
9							□		
10		☌			✱	△			☍
11	⊛		✱						
12	0h28			✱			✱		
13								△	
14									
15		✱	☌	□	☌	☍			△

Tag	☉	♇	♆	♅	♄	♃	♂	♀	☿
16	△							□	
17				△			☌		
18	☾	□						✱	□
19	18h01				✱	△			
20		△	✱						✱
21	✱			☍	□	□	✱		
22			□						
23	N				△	✱	□	☌	
24		☍	△						
25	● 9h16			△			△		☌
26									
27				□				✱	
28		△	S		☍	☌			
29	✱			✱				□	

11.Febr. Mondfinsternis 0^h40^m Weltzeit.
25.Febr. Sonnenfinsternis 9^h17^m Weltzeit, total in Nordafrika und Mittelasien.
Feb.11. Eclipse of the Moon 0^h40^m GT.
Feb.25. Eclipse of the Sun 9h17m GT., North-Africa.

Illustration 8

Tag Day	♇	♆	♅	♄	♃	♂	♀	☿
	February 1952 Februar							
	Länge — Longitude							
1.	20°♌31'	21°♎41'	10°♋46'	14°♎56'	10°♈28'	5°♏29'	5°♑53'	27°♑33'
2.	20 R 29	21 R 41	10 R 44	14 R 55	10 39	5 53	7 07	29 06
3.	20 28	21 41	10 42	14 54	10 49	6 18	8 20	0 ♒ 26
4.	20 26	21 40	10 40	14 52	11 00	6 42	9 33	2 16
5.	20 25	21 40	10 38	14 51	11 11	7 06	10 46	3 52
6.	20 23	21 40	10 36	14 50	11 22	7 30	12 00	5 29
7.	20 22	21 39	10 34	14 49	11 34	7 54	13 13	6 51
8.	20 20	21 39	10 32	14 47	11 45	8 17	14 26	8 45
9.	20 19	21 38	10 30	14 45	11 56	8 40	15 40	10 24
10.	20 18	21 37	10 29	14 44	12 08	9 05	16 53	12 04
11.	20 16	21 37	10 27	14 42	12 20	9 25	18 07	13 44
12.	20 15	21 36	10 25	14 40	12 31	9 47	19 20	15 26
13.	20 13	21 35	10 23	14 38	12 43	10 09	20 34	17 08
14.	20 12	21 35	10 22	14 36	12 55	10 30	21 47	18 51
15.	20 10	21 34	10 20	14 34	13 07	10 51	23 01	20 35
16.	20 09	21 33	10 19	14 31	13 19	11 12	24 14	22 20
17.	20 07	21 33	10 17	14 29	13 31	11 32	25 28	24 06
18.	20 06	21 32	10 16	14 27	13 44	11 52	26 41	25 53
19.	20 04	21 31	10 14	14 24	13 56	12 12	27 55	27 40
20.	20 03	21 30	10 13	14 21	14 08	12 31	29 09	29 29
21.	20 02	21 29	10 11	14 19	14 21	12 50	0 ♒ 22	1 ♓ 18
22.	20 00	21 28	10 10	14 16	14 33	13 08	1 36	3 08
23.	19 59	21 27	10 09	14 13	14 46	13 26	2 50	4 59
24.	19 57	21 26	10 08	14 10	14 59	13 44	4 03	6 51
25.	19 56	21 25	10 07	14 07	15 12	14 01	5 17	8 44
26.	19 55	21 24	10 05	14 03	15 24	14 18	6 31	10 37
27.	19 53	21 23	10 04	14 00	15 37	14 34	7 45	12 31
28.	19 52	21 22	10 03	13 57	15 50	14 50	8 58	14 25
29.	19 50	21 21	10 02	13 54	16 03	15 05	10 12	16 20
Tag Day	**Breite — Latitude**							
2.	9°N10'	1°N40'	0°N23'	2°N33'	1°S11'	1°N55'	1°N02'	1°S35'
5.	9 11	1 41	0 23	2 34	1 10	1 56	0 52	1 47
8.	9 11	1 41	0 23	2 35	1 10	1 56	0 43	1 58
11.	9 12	1 41	0 23	2 36	1 09	1 56	0 33	2 03
14.	9 12	1 41	0 23	2 36	1 08	1 57	0 24	2 05
17.	9 12	1 41	0 23	2 37	1 08	1 57	0 15	2 05
20.	9 12	1 41	0 23	2 38	1 08	1 57	0 05	2 00
23.	9 12	1 42	0 23	2 38	1 07	1 57	0 S 04	1 50
26.	9 12	1 42	0 23	2 39	1 07	1 57	0 13	1 35
29.	9 12	1 42	0 23	2 40	1 06	1 57	0 21	1 16
Tag Day	**Deklination — Declination**							
2.	23°N21'	6°S54'	23°N24'	3°S31'	3°N08'	11°S41'	22°S14'	21°S54'
5.	23 23	6 54	23 24	3 29	3 21	12 04	22 08	21 02
8.	23 24	6 53	23 25	3 27	3 35	12 27	21 57	19 57
11.	23 26	6 52	23 25	3 24	3 49	12 48	21 40	18 40
14.	23 28	6 51	23 26	3 21	4 03	13 08	21 17	17 10
17.	23 29	6 50	23 26	3 18	4 18	13 27	20 49	15 27
20.	23 31	6 49	23 26	3 14	4 32	13 45	20 15	13 32
23.	23 32	6 48	23 27	3 10	4 47	14 01	19 36	11 24
26.	23 34	6 47	23 27	3 06	5 03	14 16	18 51	9 04
29.	23 35	6 45	23 27	3 02	5 18	14 30	18 02	6 33

Illustration 8

we all know, the stellar bodies orbit in curves and not along straight lines. Therefore, in computations from 12 a.m. to 12 a.m. there are more possibilities for error than in computations using midday as starting point, where the morning positions are subtracted and the afternoon positions added.

5

Determining the Transits

N ow we can start. It is best to use a pocket calendar, or to write down the days of the month on a sheet of paper, where in each case the transits can be noted (Illustration 9).

Using the point of a pencil, we trace the degrees of the Sun, starting from eleven degrees Aquarius and going counterclockwise around the cosmogram. At thirteen degrees we find □♀. This is a square of Venus, which itself is located at 13 Scorpio 46. According to the ephemeris, the Sun is located at midday on the third at 13 Aquarius 36, and accordingly, reaches the square of Venus on the afternoon of the third.

In accordance with Illustration 9, ☉□♀ is entered in the note calendar for the third. On the fourth we have at fifteen degrees Aquarius △M, i.e. the progressing Sun reaches the trine of the Midheaven at $14^\circ 43'$. Actually, we should enter: ☉p△M r, but for the sake of simplicity we can omit p and r, if we remember that the first star is always the one in progression, and the second the radical star.

The next point of aspect again is located at twenty-seven degrees Aquarius, i.e. □☊. The Moon's Node is at 27 Taurus 22. The transit ☉□☊ should be due on the seventeenth. On the afternoon of February 19 the Sun passes over into the sign Pisces. Here, various points of aspect accumulate: trine Uranus, trine Sun-Mercury, opposite Moon, etc. We have the corresponding entries: February 21 = ☉□♅, February 22 = ☉△☿, February 23 = ☉△☉, February 24 = ☉☌☉☽, February 27 = ☉□♆♀ and ☉♂♃. Because the Sun advances by approximately one degree daily, it moves thirty minutes in a half day. Therefore, it can be quickly discovered whether a constellation is due in the morning or in the afternoon. Further entries of the solar progression can be seen in the table. The next thing to do is to take a look at Mercury, Venus, Mars, etc., in order from right to left, on the right hand side of the ephemeris. Namely, the fast moving stars form very many aspects, but are not all too effective. The duration of influence barely lasts one day. Please remember Ebertin's rule of transit:

A transit is influential only for the time it takes
the progressing star to move one degree.

It is not possible to ascertain the exact duration of influence for each stellar body because, as seen from the earth, each star moves at varying rates at different times. For example, let's take a look at the movement

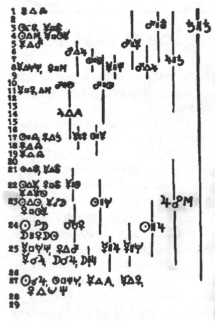

Illustration 9

of Mars. At the beginning of the month, it changes degrees every other day, then every third day, and at end of the month, every fourth day, and then to remain almost half the month of March at eighteen degrees Scorpio. It is therefore worth the while to note the duration of influence of the slow moving planets. The aspects are entered at the date due and a vertical line drawn towards top and bottom for the duration of influence. Jupiter opposite Midheaven is due on February 23. Jupiter remains five days at fourteen degrees, so we draw the vertical two days towards the top and two days towards the bottom. In this way we can obtain a clear view of the duration of the influence and potency of the constellations. Those who have worked out this example in this form will also be able to find the transits for their own cosmogram very quickly.

16

6

The Parallels

Those who have delved further into cosmobiology can use in their monthly computations the parallels. We speak of parallels when stellar bodies have the same declination, i.e. the same deviation from the equator. Taking a look at the movement of the Sun, we see that the Sun crosses the celestial equator going north (N) on the twenty-first of March every year. On the twenty-first of June the declination or deviation from the equator has reached its greatest point, $23°27'$, and the Sun starts back toward the equator, crossing it going south (S) on September 23; the greatest distance from the equator is reached on December 22 at $23°27'$S, and the return to the equator is made on March 21. Seen from the earth, the other stars follow the solar orbit, with some deviation. It is therefore very frequently the case that some stars occupy the same distance, the same declination from the equator. These stars move in parallel circles to the equator.

The ephemerides usually give the declination for three days, because the process of change is very slow. In order to observe the parallels of the progressing stars to the declinations of the radical stars, it is of course also necessary to compute the declinations for the radix, something which is very often neglected.

For the birth date October 27, 1891 there are the following declinations:

$\odot = 12°45S \quad \mathrm{24} = 9°47S$
$\mathbb{D} = 14°33N \quad \hbar = 3°32N$
$\mathbb{\breve{Y}} = 12°03S \quad \mathbb{\delta\!\!\!/} = 11°41S$

♀ = 15°32S♆ = 20°07N
♂ = 0°21S⯓ = 10°12N

Some parallels are already contained in the cosmogram itself, for example, ☉//☿, ☿//♅, ♃//⯓.

The parallels are computed in exactly the same way as the transits. In the ephemeris, we first look under the solar column under declination to see if any conformity is evident. On February 7 the Sun is at 15°33S, therefore ☉//♀. On the seventeenth the Sun is at 12°15S, ☉//☿ results.

Due to the Moon's short period of revolution, its parallels are computed only in rare cases. Because ☉//♃⯓, ☿//♃⯓ result around February 24, it is significant that on the twenty-fifth ☽//♃⯓ and ☽☌♃ are also due.

7

Mundane Aspects

The aspects which the progressing stars form beneath them, i.e. which become in each case due in space, are termed mundane aspects (mundus = world). In the ephemeris the mundane aspects are placed into two categories: 1) the "mutual aspects" of the stellar bodies, bottom left on the page of the ephemeris, and 2) the "lunar aspects," where only the aspects of the Moon to the other stellar bodies are specified, aspects which are especially numerous because of the Moon's speed. The phases of the Moon are included in the first column.

It is of special significance when mundane aspects and transits are due simultaneously in the personal cosmogram. Since, for example, Sun and Mercury are in mundane conjunction on February 22, a trine results in the cosmogram through Sun and Mercury jointly to Uranus, Mercury and the Sun. Similarly, the mundane trine of Mercury and Mars is in relation to Venus during the last days of the month.

New Moon is on the twenty-fifth, i.e. Sun and Moon are in conjunction. As can be read in the footnote at the bottom of the left hand page of the ephemeris, even a solar eclipse is due on February 25. When extraordinary events are reported, we should always take a look at the mundane aspects where we can find confirmation time and time again, especially around the time of the New or Full Moon. The solar eclipse on February 25 was total in North Africa and Central Asia. Of interest in this connection is the fact that at this time panic broke out among the natives in North Africa, great parts of Syria were overcome by severe floods, and in Iraq, locusts in swarms 70 kilometers long devastated the country. A strong earthquake occurred near Mannheim, Germany on February 24 at 22h 30m, and was thus also within the same range of influence.

8

Evaluating the Transits

There is a rule to be found in outdated books about the interpretation of aspects:

> Sextiles and trines are favorable, squares and oppositions unfavorable, conjunctions and parallels should be evaluated according to the character of the stellar body.

The so-called neutral stars Mercury and Moon supposedly take on the characteristics of the stellar body they have come into relation with. This interpretive basis can only be considered very primitive indeed. It may serve its purpose as a starting point for the beginner in astrology, but the student will soon make discoveries which are in contradiction to this method of interpretation. Practical work and experience are always the best teachers.

The most varying opinions arise from the mere speculation as to what is favorable, and what is unfavorable. Many people today consider winning the football pool as a special favor of destiny. A newspaper survey showed that only very few gained any happiness from their winnings.

In previous editions of this book the differentiation was made in the transits: f. = favorable, u. = unfavorable; the conjunctions were marked C. This division has not proven correct. The observation was very often made that squares brought about auspicious moments, and one well-known expert spoke of "the curse of the trines." This may be an exaggeration, but there are cases where trines have had very negative influence. If, for example, Saturn forms on both sides a trine to Sun and Moon, then it is at the same time placed in the middle, i.e. in the half-sum of Sun/Moon, which can be termed unfavorable. Half-sums will be treated in a chapter towards the end of this book, in the Appendix.

The categorization into positive (+), and negative (-), is also not quite correct, but yet it remains the best solution. You will often find that a positive evaluation at the same time demands a negative. A person who is happy and gay is certainly in a positive frame of mind, but here can be negative consequences if he at the same time neglects his obligations. If an impoverished, starving man is invited to a sumptuous meal, he will certainly be happy, but whether the good food will agree with him after the long period of privation is another question. A violent argument between two persons is certainly something that cannot be termed pleasant; but if this argument clears the air, and peace ensures, a state of disharmony can thus be overcome. During certain constellations many persons are full of inner tension. To achieve release, it is not necessary for an especially favorable transit to come into effect; rather, just the end of an undesirable cosmic equivalent can bring about the removal of stress. These few examples should serve to demonstrate that it is not easy to designate a constellation as favorable or unfavorable.

In most cases, not one, but several transits are due to appear at the same time, which facilitates the careful consideration of a prognostication.

Every natal chart is different, the stars have differing influences in each one. According to Parm, there are various "figurines," certain kinds of cosmograms. In the harmonious figurine, where all stars are dispersed as evenly as possible, conjunctions, for example, have negative influence, oppositions good, and trines are neutral. In the opposition figurine, where most of the stars are in opposition, the conjunctions have, in general, a good influence, oppositions are of no significance, and trines are often disharmonious. In the conjunction figurine, where most stars are clustered together in a small area of the zodiac, conjunctions are unimportant, while oppositions are critical and trines can bring about improvement. As we see, the basic cosmogram has to be examined first, and then long range observations on the transits are recorded, and thus we learn in which way the constellations act in the personal natal chart.

The author has often advocated that the "axial aspects" which derive from the "wind rose" (conjunction, square, opposition) signalize an exciting moment, i.e. something is happening, while the tripartite aspects (sextile, trine), denote a state of condition.

In other words, the sextiles and trines indicate what life offers; the conjunctions, square and oppositions reveal what life demands. The problem can be approached from any side whatever, lengthy dissertations can be written on it, and one can only come to this conclusion:

> The effect of the cosmic constellation is dependent on the character and behavior of man himself.

If astrology is not only to be construed as the interpretation of the stellar constellation for the purpose of a prognostication of the future, if the true aim of cosmobiology is the correlation of the cosmos and the living creature, then a stellar constellation is not alone the essence of the cosmos. Then:

1. An individual is the product of generations, man carries within himself hereditary factors which, corresponding to the cosmic constellations, will take effect in life. Good or bad hereditary factors cannot be seen from the cosmogram alone, but rather, solely in a comparison to the cosmograms of the parents and family.

2. Landscape and climate can give a completely different turn to the effects of the transits. Not only the location of the place of birth is a determining factor, but also the respective whereabouts of a person. Whether a person is in his homeland, in the tropics, at sea, or near the polar region under critical constellations, the possible effects on health, frame of mind, and attitude towards other persons are everywhere varied, even if a general tendency can be traced.

3. The environment in its various forms can hardly be deduced from the natal chart. What we term environment is firstly the narrow circle in which an individual moves: his home, his family, his work (school, institute, factory, team, association, etc.) place of residence (village, town, city, country) and landsmen. Many persons are easily influenced by their environment, others are able to exert an influence on the environment. The relationship between individual and environment is variable from instance to instance, and, here, the respective constellations play a great role. An individual has another relation to his environment under a Saturn constellation as when under a Jupiter constellation.

4. The conditions of life are compounded not only from the environment, but also from upbringing, from schooling, vocation, financial situation in the home, and from personal activities. The effects of certain constellations will be different in the case of a laborer from those of an industrialist or a minister of state; the poor, the rich, craftsmen and

intellectual workers will experience varying constellation effects.

5. An important factor in the varying kinds of behavior under different constellations is an individual's philosophy of life. According to whether he has been raised as a Catholic, Protestant, Buddhist or Mohammedan, or has become a convert some time in his life, a person will react differently.

6. The stages of development vary from person to person. A child will behave differently under certain circumstances from an adolescent, an adult, or an elderly person in the very same circumstances. A critical Saturn position can mean for a young man fleeting illness, but for an old man, death. A child's joy over a toy can be triggered by a good Jupiter transit, and which would mean for young persons some shared happiness, or for an older individual new perception.

7. The decisive factor in every reaction to cosmic influence is the individual himself. The development of a person correlates in manifold respects to the cosmic rhythms, be they of the Sun, Moon, Uranus, or Saturn, the parallels are there. The real purpose of a prognostication is to find the correct correlations in practical life to the cosmos, to utilize favorable periods properly and better to overcome critical times. The point is not to figure out great profits, but to recognize those times when something can be undertaken with the least risk in order to achieve success. Achieving the Big Win by astrological calculation is not possible, otherwise all astrologers would be rich men. Calculations can only be made of the possibilities for success, but all such possibilities cannot become fact because man is caught in a complicated steel web of multifarious influences; of these the cosmic factor and perhaps the individual's own willpower are known, but there is a multitude of factors which remain unknown.

Even if we are conscious of the limits set to a prognostication, there are still ample advantages to be offered by the application of cosmobiology to practical life. Although not everything can be read from the transits and other methods of calculation have to be employed, even the knowledge of a favorable period lying before him gives a person stimulus, confidence and incentive, so that success is almost a sure thing. It is most certainly important to know weeks, months, or even years in advance when there is a favorable period of time for taking up a profession, for taking an examination, for opening a business, for undertaking a change in vocation or residence. However, it is also of equal importance to know when checks, difficulties or impairment of health may be due, to know when it is hard to keep in touch with people, when estrangement or separation are possible. The possible consequences will become clearer if the head of the family considers not only his own natal chart, but also that of his wife and children. How very difficult it is at times to understand and estimate correctly a small child who has not yet learned to talk. If a crisis of health is anticipated, a diet for prevention can be set up. The possibilities of accident can be recognized ahead of time; and under favorable transits, joy is great when the child makes good progress in its development.

If in the interpretation of transits we start from the assumption that an individual with his own willpower determines to a great extent the manifestation of the constellations, and through the transits themselves is conscious of the potentialities and the limits of a prognostication for the future in all circumstances, then this person, after a period of observation and experience, will be able to pilot his own way through life with greater assurance and success. The way a person applies astrology depends on his ethical views and his moral development. The stars cannot be held responsible for the consequences of the improper use of astrology, only the individual himself is at fault.

A differentiation must first be made between the transits, a differentiation between strong and weak ones, between those which can bring about a change in life, and those which merely have a hand in shaping ordinary, everyday life. The slower a stellar body moves, the stronger its influence. Whoever has stood under the influence of the transits of Pluto, Neptune or Uranus will hardly be able to say he "has felt nothing." The Sun often leads to a triggering of stronger transits. The Moon moves too fast to be recognized each time in its correspondence. But whoever has a cluster of planets in his natal chart will notice when the Moon is just crossing these points. Mercury and Venus also move relatively fast, so that their manifestations are also not always ascertainable. Mars, on the other hand, is certainly more perceptible; those who have experienced great excitement, an accident, or have undergone similar strain, will often note that Mars participated in these events. Moreover, Mars frequently is effective one or two days before actual transit, while most effects usually take shape on or at the mean due dates of the various transits. Jupiter is usually overestimated in its effect; more is expected of its good transits than is possible. It all depends on whether, according to the ephemeris, Jupiter is apparently moving very fast or slow. Saturn is almost always felt in its oppressing, restricting or separating manifestation; Uranus often brings about great upheavals in life; Neptune brings nerve-racking times; and Pluto brings about a connection to the mass fate of contemporary generations or leads to unusual occurrences.

Every reader should first impress these basics on his mind and use these general tendencies as guidelines for interpretation. The reader will get farther by doing this than by concentrating on details from the very first.

Furthermore, it is essential to consider the character of the stellar bodies.

9

Character of the Stellar Bodies

It is essential to consider the character of the stellar bodies as factors of interpretation more closely:

Sun: Creative spirit, the excitement of life, the male, heart, day.

Moon: The soul, fertility, the female, mutability, the bodily liquids, night.

Mercury: The mind, thinking, intellect, science, commerce, nerves, language.

Venus: Love, attraction, beauty, art, joy, harmony, virginity.

Mars: Drive, desire, energy, willpower, action, activity, effort.

Jupiter: Satisfaction, happiness, wealth, luck, morality, ethics, law, community, family, marriage.

Saturn: Restriction, organic as well as psychological inhibitions, experience, concentration, mental and emotional pain, separation, grief.

Uranus: Suddenness, release of tensions, excitement, emotion, rebellion, reform, inventions, intuition.

Neptune: Receptivity, susceptibility, deception, disorganization, paralysis, wearing down, psychoses.

Pluto: Force majeure, providence, power, the masses, transformation, change.

Moon's Node: Associations with other persons, sexual connections, fellowship, cooperation.

Ascendant: Environment, behavior towards other persons, development of the personality.

Midheaven: Ego, individuality, aim of life.

Those who note these basic interpretations will also be able to take up the combination of the various interpretive factors, i.e. the combination of Sun and Moon pertains to male and female, parents, marriage, or, too, body and soul, spirit and temper. Mars and Saturn result in energy and restraint and can therefore also bring about tension, conflict, difficulties, antagonism. Jupiter and Mars can be termed planets of happiness or success (Jupiter), and of energy (Mars). Refer to *The Combination of Stellar Influences*.

For the recognition of positive (+) or negative (-), favorable or unfavorable, constructive or destructive, joining or separating characteristics, the following table should serve as a guide. The question mark (?) indicates those cases where a clear-cut difference between + and - cannot be made.

☉ : ☽ +	☉ : ☿ +	☉ : ♀ +	☉ : ♂ ?	☉ : ♃ +	☉ : ♄ -
☉ : ♅ -	☉ : ♆ -	☉ : ☊ ?	☉ : ♇ -	☉ : A +	☉ : M +
☽ : ☿ +	☽ : ♀ +	☽ : ♂ ?	☽ : ♃ +	☽ : ♄ -	☽ : ♅ -
☽ : ♆ -	☽ : ♇ -	☽ : ☊ ?	☽ : A ?	☽ : M ?	☿ : ♀ +
☿ : ♂ -	☿ : ♃ +	☿ : ♄ -	☿ : ♅ -	☿ : ♆ -	☿ : ♇ -
☿ : ☊ ?	☿ : A +	☿ : M +	♀ : ♂ ?	♀ : ♃ +	♀ : ♄ -
♀ : ♅ ?	♀ : ♆ -	♀ : ♇ -	♀ : ☊ ?	♀ : A +	♀ : M +
♂ : ♃ +	♂ : ♄ -	♂ : ♅ -	♂ : ♆ -	♂ : ♇ -	♂ : ☊ -
♂ : A -	♂ : M +	♃ : ♄ -	♃ : ♅ +	♃ : ♆ ?	♃ : ♇ ?
♃ : A +	♃ : M +	♃ : ☊ +	♄ : ♅ -	♄ : ♆ -	♄ : ♇ -
♄ : ☊ -	♄ : A -	♄ : M -	♅ : ♆ -	♅ : ♇ -	♅ : ☊ -
♅ : A -	♅ : M -	♆ : ♇ -	♆ : ☊ -	♆ : A -	♆ : M -
♇ : ☊ -	♇ : A -	♇ : M -	☊ : A +	☊ : M +	

This table is primarily to be used for squares and oppositions.

10

The Interpretation of the Monthly Prognostication

Those who have delved more deeply into cosmobiology will first calculate the directions and transits for an entire year, will ascertain the annual tendency and, finally, will investigate each month individually. The novice in these studies who wants to progress step by step will begin with a survey of the transits for one month. It would not be correct to consider February 1 and then to look for what Mercury trine Moon's Node means; and then February 2 would be taken up and the correlations of Saturn parallel Saturn looked up.

This sort of method of observation can be compared to the flower lover who crouches on the ground looking at one flower after another, and thereby completely missing the wealth of color and the splendid variety of this carpet of flowers, an impression he would get by looking at his garden as a whole.

First the whole must be taken, and only then can the details be considered, otherwise the coherence and interrelationship of the compounding elements cannot be grasped. It should not be expected that every constellation will manifest exactly on the day it falls due; rather, its effect will generally show up amidst several transits.

Orienting ourselves according to the vertical lines, Saturn parallel Saturn first strikes the eye, and signifies a period of restriction. Because the due date of this transit is at the beginning of the month, its effect will diminish towards the middle and end of the month. Mars trine

Jupiter serves around February 8 as a good counterbalance, even though Jupiter parallel Saturn will still be able to bring about a period of indecisiveness and lack initiative. Around the middle of the month, Jupiter enters a trine to the Ascendant.

Those transits, as personal points of the natal chart, of the Midheaven, Ascendant, Sun and Moon, can be designated as especially strong, because they apply not to that great circle of persons born on this day, but rather to those who on this day first saw the light of the world at a particular hour and minute, and at a particular joy or happiness in their environment (Ascendant).

The number of constellations increases towards the end of the month. Here, ♃☍M is particularly predominant. According to the old method of interpretation, an opposition would be unfavorable. However, if we combine the basic interpretations: Jupiter = joy, happiness, MC = the ego, aim in life, we can only speak here of joy and happiness, applying to one person alone. In addition, follow ☉//♃ and , ☽//♀☉♃, denoting a woman's joy, and following these are weaker transits which lie with the same range of interpretation as ☿☌ and //♃. These propitious constellations are grouped around February 24. On this day, the native won 2,544 deutschmarks in the football pool.

The weaker transits of the proximate days are completely overshadowed by the continuing constellations. Of course, clues to the event can be had from the diurnal constellations. On February 21, under Sun and Mercury in trine to Uranus, she must have had the right idea occur to her about how to fill out her football pool ticket; under Sun trine Mercury and Mercury trine Sun/Mercury she acted and submitted her ticket; Mars conjunct Venus and Sun opposite Moon brought about excitement and suspense until she learned of her luck.

We would be mistaken in saying that the constellations could have indicated her winning. The fact is that we can only see from the transits that this woman would experience a special joy or happiness at this period of time, brought about by winning the football pool. The result could have been different. The football pool has existed only for a few years; therefore, this constellation would not have resolved in the same way at an earlier date. It would perhaps have been winning the lottery, or perhaps a special gift, or moving into a new and lovely home. These remarks are only to show that it is not possible to tie oneself to the details in such a prognostication. Instead, one can only see the indications of a particular destiny, the possibilities or tendencies. Under such a constellation one does not perforce win the football pool, but rather, one might win.

The best thing to do in order to obtain a proper survey of the month is to use a colored pencil and underline the aspects we consider favorable in blue and the others in red. In those cases where we are not sure, it is better to omit the underlining.

This example has already been treated by Georg Hoffman in the journal "Kosmobiologie," and he found that several directions had accumulated in the years 1950 to 1952, which were triggered by transits. Namely, this woman not only won once, but twelve times, and this although in the years preceding she never had any luck at all in gambling.

For the first example the monthly prognostication has purposely been derived solely from the transits themselves, i.e. from the aspects of the stellar bodies in progression to the positions of the basic cosmogram. Most books in this field attempt to determine the event itself by using further interpretive factors. In the previous editions of this book, the following points were also brought to the reader's special attention:

1. The nature of the planets in progression (the transiting body). In our example, progressing Jupiter, which is generally counted as a planet of happiness, is the prime key.

2. The nature of the zodiacal sign in which the progressing body or transiting body is positioned. In February 1952, Jupiter is in the sign Aries, where it can bring about an optimistic attitude and spirit of enterprise. We should remember, however, that winning is possible at all times, irrespective of which sign Jupiter occupies. Therefore, the nature of the stellar body itself seems to be of greater significance than that of the sign.

3. The kind of house in which a stellar body makes station. The progressing Jupiter is at the cusp of the fourth house, which applies to the parental home and the person's own home, according to the system of houses. One may certainly say that, here, Jupiter brought luck to this woman's home. Otherwise, the fifth house is known to be decisive in matters of gambling, lottery, and speculation. The fifth house has no part in this case.

4. The kind of aspect the progressing planet forms. Jupiter is in opposition to the Midheaven. Usually, opposition connotes misfortune, but here it brought good luck because this was a connection between Jupiter and the Midheaven, of luck and individual. Of course, one could object and say that Jupiter is conjunct the cusp of the fourth house, and therefore, brought about this domestic happiness. But, as a matter of principle, we should leave aside such matters of dispute and, instead, resolve to make our own observations and to gain our own experience.

5. The nature of the aspected radical point. The Midheaven pertains here to ego, personal experience.

6. The character of the sign in which the aspected point is located. The sign Libra is doubtless of lesser significance than the Midheaven

itself. However, we could apply a somewhat artificial interpretation and say that the sign Libra is decisive for conjugality and public affairs, and that, in this case, the family state of happiness was affected by good fortune as triggered by a public occurrence.

7. The character of the house in which the aspected point is located. According to the old rule, Jupiter, in order to be decisive for speculative profits, has to be located in the fifth house. In this case, there is no planet at all in this sector. The Midheaven is regarded as the cusp of the tenth house, which is decisive primarily for vocation. Winning the lottery, however, has nothing whatever to do with the profession. This win is no success because in the real sense of the word, success is the result of work done well, but not of lucky speculation.

George Hoffman also pointed out in his article on this case that this natal chart did not bring any confirmation of the significance of the houses. One should endeavor with prognostication to make the most of small means. The more factors one takes into consideration, the more complicated becomes the interpretation, and the few factors applied, the more clear-cut the overall view.

11

Sensitive Points and Half-Sums

According to astrological tradition the transits are also investigated by way of the sensitive points, i.e. a combination of certain stellar bodies with the Ascendant. The "Wheel of Fortune," for example, can be derived when the distance of the Sun and Moon to the Ascendant is added; the "Cross," as the point of disease and death, by adding the difference of Mars and Saturn to the Ascendant; and the "Heart," as point for love and marriage, from the distance of Sun and Venus to the Ascendant. There are many other sensitive points used in calculation, but which become of no use when the time of birth is not precise to the minute, resulting in the Ascendant being changed by a few degrees.

Alfred Witte, founder of the Hamburg School of Astrology, introduced into astrology some decades ago the use of half-sums, which are the midpoints between each pair of planets, and hence are also called half-distance points, bisecting, or mixed points. The application of the half-sums is for the novice cosmobiologist a bit difficult at the beginning, for which reason only short mention is made of these here. For detailed treatment of half-sums please refer to my book *Charakter und Schicksal im Kosmogramm* and *The Combination of Stellar Influences*. Also very instructive is the cosmobiological study of a tragedy of love in the "Kosmische Ehe." In this example the following constellations, among others, are due:

Uranus p 3 Taurus 31 opposite Sun p 3 Scorpio 21 with Moon at 4 Scorpio 28 (New Moon) signify in themselves an exciting event (Uranus) between male (Sun) and female (Moon). In the female natal chart, this mundane (earthly) position coincides with Mars at 4 Scorpio 54, which in itself already indicates an act (Mars) of violence (Uranus). In the female cosmogram, Saturn is at 5 Virgo 26 and Moon at 3 Capricorn 13. The midpoint, or half-sum, of these two stellar bodies is therefore at approximately four degrees Scorpio, where Mars is located in the natal chart. This point is also in square to the half-sum Uranus/Ascendant (Uranus = 4 Pisces 15, Ascendant = 5 Capricorn 09, the half-sum Uranus/Ascendant is therefore approximately four to five degrees Aquarius square Mars). According to *The Combination of Stellar Influences*, Mars = Uranus/Ascendant, for example, means: to be threatened, injured or wounded. This young woman was murdered by her lover on the corresponding day.

The use of half-sums makes for great precision in calculation and also more exact interpretation, so that after mastering the use of transits, going on to the consideration of half-sums is highly recommended.

12

Paying Attention to Medium Coeli and Ascendant

Paying attention to the Medium Coeli (Midheaven) and Ascendant is very important. When a progressing planet is in the vicinity of the Ascendant and Midheaven, attention should be paid to when a constellation forms. You should note, for example, what effects the transit of Mars, Jupiter, Saturn, Uranus, etc. has brought about, and then compute the positions down to the exact minute of the stellar bodies at this moment. By virtue of numerous conformities, the exact value for the Ascendant and Midheaven can be quickly obtained, on the basis of which a more exact prognostication can be formulated.

As long as the Ascendant and Midheaven have not been ascertained, it is advisable in each case to extend the radius of influence of the transits. Certainly, difficulties will arise when other stellar bodies are located very near the Ascendant or Midheaven in the cosmogram, so that it is not always easy to say whether an event has been triggered off by a transit over the Ascendant and Midheaven or over the corresponding stellar body. A result can be obtained here through continuous observation and the precise definition of occurrences.

13

Which Is the Best Day to Realize Plans?

The whole idea behind observing the transits is of course the sense of being in harmony with the cosmos, of directing one's life in line with the cosmic correspondence, but this without becoming a slave to the stellar influence. The first differentiations to be made are those between favorable and unfavorable, positive and negative constellations. Under a beneficial Jupiter transit, one will be enterprising, and under a poor Saturn aspect, one will have to face up to a greater expenditure of energy in order to overcome difficulties. Bit by bit, the attempt can be made to connect individual transits with particular kinds of plans.

Intellectual work requires good transits of or to Mercury (the mind), Neptune (inspiration, imagination, and fantasy), Uranus (intuition, constructiveness), Saturn (concentration), or Venus (art).

Physical work is sooner crowned with success under transits of or to Mars (energy), the Sun (the body), the Sun to Mars = physical strength, Saturn (patience, endurance), Uranus (drive), or Mercury (intellectually directed strength).

Vocation, entrance into a profession, and aim in life depend on their relationship to the Midheaven; in part, too, to the Ascendant when this entails at the same time an influence on the environment as, for example, in the case of a craftsman; promotion (Jupiter to the Sun, Mercury, Ascendant, Midheaven; Saturn to the Sun, Mercury, Ascendant, Midheaven); negotiations with a superior (Jupiter to the Sun, Jupiter, Ascendant, Midheaven); change of occupation (Uranus to the Ascendant, Midheaven, Sun, Mercury).

Marriage especially demands great attention paid to the transits to Sun (male) and Moon (female); to factors concerning sexual relationship; Mars, Venus (sexual drive) and Moon's Node (sexual relationship); to those of Jupiter (happiness and harmony) and the personal points Ascendant and Midheaven.

Friendship and acquaintanceship between male and female evolve under transits of Jupiter to the Sun, Moon, Ascendant, Midheaven, Venus, Mars; under those of Uranus (sudden relations) to the Sun, Moon, Ascendant, Midheaven, Venus, Mars, Moon's Node. Neptune plays a big part in evoking disappointments and errors; Saturn leads to estrangement and separation.

Profits through the lottery, football pool, and speculation in general result primarily under Jupiter transits in association with Uranus (sudden good fortune), with Neptune (hoped for luck, speculation, profit without performance of work), with Ascendant and Midheaven (personal happiness).

Change in location and residence are furthered under transits of Uranus to Ascendant and Midheaven, and also to Mercury, Jupiter, and Saturn.

Court trials are easier won when conducted under transits of Jupiter. Jupiter trine Mars is especially favorable, but Jupiter square and opposite Mars frequently lead to favorable decisions as well.

Examinations should be taken under beneficial transits of Jupiter, Uranus, or even Saturn.

Trips for recreation will turn out well if Jupiter is positioned favorably in respect to Mercury, Uranus, Saturn, and, in the case of ocean voyage, Neptune often plays a role.

14

Basic Interpretation----The Sun

The Sun is the giver of life, lending man physical, mental and spiritual strength.

Psychological Correspondence
+ Will to live, joy of life, desire for power, magnanimity.
- Lack of will to live and of willpower, indecisiveness, extravagance, arrogance.

Biological Correspondence
Health, vital energy, heart, circulation, (brain, right eye of males, left eye of females, right side of body); heart diseases, eye disease, nervous disorder, convulsions.

Sociological Correspondence
Male, father, civil servants, persons of authority.

Duration of Transit Influence
One to two days.

Transits of the Sun
1. Sun to Sun
    + (C) Harmony in body and spirit.
    - Ill-health.
2. Sun to Moon
    + Mental balance, good humor, pleasant contact, good relations with the other sex.
    - Inner dissatisfaction, instability of character, conflict of interests

and obligations, tendency towards spiritual conflict, impairment of health (especially true of women).

3. Sun to Mercury
   + (C) Practical thinking, clear intellect, consciousness of goals, organizational talent. Favorable for matters of business, negotiations, correspondence, short trips, acquaintanceships.
   - Obscurity, absentmindedness, disinclination to work, bad humor because of letters or negotiations.

4. Sun to Venus
   + (C) Amorous feelings, power of attraction, popularity, affection, sense of art, expression of emotional and love life, small successes or gifts.
   - Uncontrolled love drive, disharmony, appearances exceed inner value, pleasure seeking, needless expenditure.

5. Sun to Mars
   + Energy, resoluteness, creative power, instinct, courage, ambition, striving for power, chances for success.
   - (C) Rashness, irritation, obstinacy, impulsiveness, quarrelsomeness, inclination to illness and mishap. In case of illness, high temperature. Extravagant demands, overstrain.

6. Sun to Jupiter
   + (C) Good health, striving for power and possession, recognition, success in negotiations (with authorities), social sense, sociability, joy, pleasure, small gifts.
   - Conflicts arising from arrogant and pretentious behavior, negligence, extravagance, needless expense, illness through improper nutrition, conflict with superiors or persons of authority, difference of opinion in contractual matters.

7. Sun to Saturn
   + Quiet, persistence, absorption, self-assertion, seclusion, modesty, creative endurance, concentration, contact with older persons, getting ahead gradually.
   - (C) Weak constitution, enforced modesty and reserve, restrictions and difficulties, tendency to pessimism.

8. Sun to Uranus
   + Inclination to change and reform, new plans, surprise visits or sudden news, love of freedom, versatility, intuition.
   - (C) Sudden hindrance of plans, small setbacks, sudden disharmony in love life.

9. Sun to Neptune
   + Receptivity to all impressions, vivid imagination, enthusiasm, tendency to mysticism, profundity, liking for travel, empathy.

Little success in money matters.
- (C) Impressionability, disappointments, plans without possibility of realization, inclination to alcohol, nicotine, etc., self-delusion, deceit, enmities.
10. Sun to Pluto
   + Striving for power, desire to be superior to others, leading and influencing others, self-assertion.
   - (C) Having to submit, misguided fanaticism, arrogance, over-estimation of self.
11. Sun to Moon's Node
   + (C) Desire for association and acquaintanceship, mutual experiences, cooperation, fellowship, public relations.
   - Cooperation made difficult, disturbance of associations, separation.
12. Sun to Ascendant
   + (C) Positive attitude towards environment, attainment of recognition, public relations, desire to be important.
   - Disharmonious relation with the environment, being placed at a disadvantage by others, estrangement.
13. Sun to Midheaven
   + (C) Consciousness of goal, industry and diligence, development of personality, recognition of one's mission, positive attitude towards life, occupational advantages.
   - Obscure goals, aimlessness, wrong attitude towards life, disinclination to work.

Practical Examples

If the Sun alone is effective as a transit, then no strong correspondence will result; of concern here are only matters of ordinary daily life, things that most persons hardly even notice.

For example, under Sun trine Venus, a young man will meet with his female friend, or a woman receives a love letter; under Sun trine Mars an office worker will be able to do his job well and will receive due recognition; under Sun conjunct Saturn a writer in seclusion will be able to concentrate on his work, whereas on this same day he would otherwise have to overcome difficulties and hindrances in public life; one man cuts himself while shaving under Sun opposition Mars and is annoyed because he has to go to a dinner with a cut on his face.

One young man wrote in a letter once about Sun square Mars: "On a Monday night, as this transit was due, I dreamed that I was on my wedding trip with Miss X, and was very excited erotically, so that I woke up. I went back to sleep and slept soundly, but I was still very excited the whole day and could only get over it by exerting great self-control.''

Under Sun square Saturn a fourteen-year-old boy saw how his parents quarreled, and how his mother degraded his father and called him all sorts of bad names, causing the boy great anguish because he loved his father very much.

A solar transit alone will rarely be manifest in an event; usually, several transits are due where the Sun acts as trigger. Above all, the natal chart must be examined as a whole. In this examination one must take into consideration whether or not the point transited by the Sun has multiple links to other points of the natal chart through aspects or constellation.

15

Basic Interpretation----The Moon

The Moon represents the imperfect and mutable. It especially relates to the soul and the feminine principle, and to the emotions and instincts of the individual. As a Full Moon it is especially intense and stimulating in its influence, whereas as a New Moon it has a weakening effect.

Psychological Correspondence
+ Motherliness, domesticity, caution, versatility, desire for change, accommodation, benevolence.
- Suppressed motherliness, indolence, impressionability, carelessness, moodiness, vacillation, pretence, lying.

Biological Correspondence
Fertility, system of bodily fluids, stomach, left eye of men, right eye of women, sexual organs. Menstruation and the various stages of motherhood are particularly subject to lunar influence. Temporary paralysis and illnesses of short duration, catarrh, emotional disturbance.

Sociological Correspondence
Mother, wife, woman, family, landsmen, hereditary factors, feminine persons, persons such as travelers, seamen, messengers.

Duration of Transit Influence
Two to three hours.

Transits of the Moon
14. Moon to Sun

+ Amorous affection, visits, small gifts, advantages, recognition and
praise.
- Disharmonious love life, changes in mood, ill health.
C Usually favorable for male in respect to love life; for female, slight
ill health.
15. Moon to Moon
+ (C) Pleasant mood, relation to women.
- Changes in mood.
16. Moon to Mercury
+ (C) Intellectual stimulation, small transactions, slight changes,
acquaintanceships, associations, news, letters, short trips.
- Disinclination to work, nervousness, dispute, inclination to head-
aches.
17. Moon to Venus
+ (C) Gay mood, feelings of love, desire for affection, sociability,
sound judgment of the material things in life, of advantage in the
purchase of clothes and jewelry.
- Small disputes with women, moodiness, impressionability, sexual
excitement, ill health due to overeating and drinking, gossip.
18. Moon to Mars
+ Impulsiveness, consciousness of goals, acting on emotions, enterprise, small successes.
- (C) Unmotivated acts, excited mood, rashness, rebellion, quarrel-
some, irritable.
19. Moon to Jupiter
+ (C) Feeling of happiness, obliging, helpfulness, kindness, small
advantages, visits, gifts, recognition, favorable for negotiations
with superiors and civil authorities.
- Indifference, negligence, inner conflict, unpleasant visits, differences with superiors, tendency toward needless expenditure.
20. Moon to Saturn
+ Self-control, circumspection, sense of duty, settling matters of
importance. Good for working in seclusion and for negotiations
with older persons.
- (C) Taciturn, sense of inferiority, slight inhibitions, small difficulties, estrangement, lack of self-confidence, fear of exposure, weak
constitution.
21. Moon to Uranus
+ Intensified emotional excitability, ambition, acting on instinct,
self-will, surprises, unusual experiences.
- Obstinacy, narrow minded, fanaticism, exaggeration, nervous
tension, restlessness, need for sensation; disputes arising from

rashness.

C Tendency toward extravagant acts, excess.

22. Moon to Neptune

+ Delicacy, introspection, intense dream life, intellectual stimulation, mystic experiences.

- Illusion, self-delusion, instability, given to lying, defamation, sleeplessness.

C Not being understood, dissatisfaction, inclined to overenjoyment of alcohol, nicotine, etc.

23. Moon to Pluto

+ Fanatic pursuance of certain aims, power of assertion.

- (C) Sudden outburst of emotion, strong excitability of individual complexes of emotion.

24. Moon to Moon's Node

+ (C) Spiritual relationship, attitude toward other persons based on the spirit, relations with women.

- Interruption of spiritual contact.

25. Moon to Ascendant

+ (C) Harmonious attitude toward other persons, aptitude for making acquaintances.

- Disharmonious relation to the environment.

26. Moon to Midheaven

+ (C) Search for spiritual understanding, heartfelt affection.

- Vacillation of affections, changing goals.

Practical Examples

If several stellar bodies are clustered together in a natal chart, thereby being in mutual contact with the Moon, every time the Moon crosses this point, similar feelings or moods or events will recur; that is to say, a certain periodicity of seven, fourteen, twenty-one or twenty-eight days will result.

One woman, in whose natal chart four stellar bodies were positioned in Sagittarius, reports that she is always very irritable when under a bad aspect of the Moon to Sagittarius. All her relations keep out of her way in order to avoid any quarrels or misunderstandings. On such days, she suffers not only from these bad moods, but also tends to illness. From her other letters: "Just lately, I had a favorable Jupiter position. At the very hour when the transiting Moon was conjunct the natal Moon, a woman came for a visit and because of previous favors brought me a lovely silhouette picture."

"When I have Moon trine Jupiter I usually receive stimulating letters or small gifts." "Once I had an accident with my bicycle. It happened at the very moment of the Moon's crossing Uranus. At the same time,

Mercury was conjunct Uranus."

Just what effect the Moon as transit has depends on how the Moon is positioned in the basic horoscope. Another woman reports: "I find poor lunar aspects to be extremely unpleasant. This probably comes from the Saturn-Moon conjunction in the basic horoscope." "We recently lost our luggage key under Moon conjunct Neptune. It was gone three days and was found again as the Moon was trine Uranus."

Due to the fact that the Moon's influence lasts only a few hours, its function is primarily that of a trigger to moods and events which are indicated by stronger transits. In general, great importance cannot be attached to the individual lunar transits. It is, however, very interesting to observe changing moods under the lunar transits and to see small setbacks and disturbances arise, how contact with others can be interrupted, or, just at the moment of a lunar transit, business livens, visitors come and go, special news is received, etc.

16

Basic Interpretation----Mercury

Mercury is the planet of the intellect, of profession, business affairs, of mediation.

Psychological Correspondence
+ Good powers of judgment, criticism, skill in expression and writing, mediation, diplomacy, intellectual ambition.
- Lack of judgment and objective criticism, intemperance, nervousness, inconstancy, lies, slyness.

Biological Correspondence
Nerve functions, nervousness.

Sociological Correspondence
Intellectual workers, tradesmen, mediators, young people, office workers, persons with dubious vocations.

Duration of Transit Influence
One to three days.

Transits of Mercury
27. Mercury to Sun
+ (C) Desire to do intellectual work, creativity, intellectual curiosity, good for negotiations, short trips, correspondence, organization, advertisement.
- Obscurity, absentmindedness, nervousness, disinclination to work, poor atmosphere for negotiations.
28. Mercury to Moon

+ (C) Intellectual stimulation, ideas and plans, small changes, negotiations. New acquaintanceships or associations. Letters, travel.
- Bad humor, disinclination to work, irritability. Disputes with women. Slight setbacks, gossip, lies.

29. Mercury to Mercury
+ (C) Good comprehension, intellectual stimulation, ease of word and expression.
- Lack of objectivity, bad humor through correspondence or visits.

30. Mercury to Venus
+ (C) Emotionally accentuated intellect, take-it-easy attitude toward life, levity, thoughts of love, love of art and beauty. Relationships with women, affection, visits, sociability, recuperation.
- Pleasure seeking, luxury, extravagance, inordinacy, disputes with women.

31. Mercury to Mars
+ Realization of ideas, active intellect, spirit of enterprise, quick settling of affairs.
- (C) Hastiness, inordinacy, restlessness, harping and nagging, nervousness, dispute.

32. Mercury to Jupiter
+ (C) Constructive intellect, wealth of thought, optimism, advantageous acquaintanceships or business transactions, successful contact with authorities, advantages of many kinds. Favorable for negotiations, contracts.
- Thoughtlessness, unreliability, exaggeration (bluffing), tactlessness, unlawful acts, conflict.

33. Mercury to Saturn
+ Good powers of concentration, perseverance, thoroughness, diligence, philosophical thinking, relations with older persons.
- (C) Inhibitions, mistrust, depressed mood, difficult working conditions, inclination to selfishness. Slight ill health, headache.

34. Mercury to Uranus
+ Perspicacity, good powers of observation, new perceptions, revolutionary ideas, unusual fields of interest, desire for independence, versatility, love of sports, travel.
- (C) Intemperance, nervous haste, rashness, unpleasant events, spoiling of plans, unwelcome visits, dispute.

35. Mercury to Neptune
+ Rich imagination, fantasy, tendency to follow up sudden ideas, inspiration, premonition of coming events, comprehension of things on an intellectual and spiritual plane.
- (C) Self-delusion, confusion, incorrect behavior, mental depres-

sion, trouble due to others.

36. Mercury to Pluto
   + Desire to persuade and influence others, striving for general recognition.
   - (C) Over-eagerness, fanaticism, over-estimation of powers of self, nervousness.

37. Mercury to Moon's Node
   + (C) Seeking or giving impulse, desire for contact, mutual interests.
   - Making oneself unpopular, antisocial attitude, dislikes.

38. Mercury to Ascendant
   + (C) Attitude toward other persons, desire to get together with others, exchange of ideas.
   - Negative attitude toward other persons, passing false judgment.

39. Mercury to Midheaven
   + (C) Ambition, love of work.
   - Vocational insecurity, obscure attitude, lack of self-criticism.

Practical Examples

The deciding factor with the Mercury transits is whether Mercury at the time is moving apparently fast or slow. At times, Mercury will remain for days at almost the same degree, and its influence is therefore greater; Mercury will sometimes also travel one degree within a period of a half day, and its influence is then correspondingly weaker. The Mercury transits belong to those constellations having a triggering effect rather than one causing moods and events.

Here are a few extracts from letters: "I achieved a noticeable monetary gain under Mercury conjunct Jupiter." "Mercury conjunct Uranus meant for me the beginning of labor pains and continual pain." "Under Mercury trine Uranus I paid a visit to a critic who later wrote a particularly good review of my production." "I was very creative under Mercury trine Saturn; I could concentrate very well, giving great impulse to my work."

17

Basic Interpretation----Venus

Venus is the planet of love and of "minor joys." We are indebted to her for the little joys of life and happy hours of pleasure.

Psychological Correspondence
+ Affection, erotic attraction, sense of harmony, beauty and art, sociability.
- Erotic aberrations, sentimentality, bad taste, carelessness, waste.

Biological Correspondence
Sexuality, secretive glands, kidneys, veins. Venereal disease, emotional disturbances, throat disease, stomach disorders (due to overeating).

Sociological Correspondence
Girl, woman, lover, wife, mother, female office workers, all persons concerned with physical well being, with the fabrication or sale of clothing, or who entertain, artists.

Duration of Transit Influence
One to three days.

Transits of Venus
40. Venus to Sun
+ (C) Affection, feeling of love, popularity, artistic stimulation, sociability, comfort, visits, small gifts and favors, liking for the high life.
- Uncontrolled amorousness, disharmony, inclination to extrava-

gance, being unsatisfied, unnecessary expenditure, disinclination, moodiness, ill health due to overeating and drinking.

41. Venus to Moon
    + (C) Content, liking for quiet and comfort, love, sociability, visits, pleasurable events, good relations with women.
    - Disagreements, disputes with women, conflict in love life, ill health due to overeating and drinking, gossip.

42. Venus to Mercury
    + (C) Emotionally accentuated intellect, taking life easy, levity, thoughts of love, relations with women, visits, sociability, recuperation, humor.
    - Pleasure seeking, luxury, extravagance, inordinacy, disputes with women, rumor, slander.

43. Venus to Venus
    + (C) Affection, good humor, stimulation, sociability, sense of beauty and art, tendency to purchases in clothes and jewelry.
    - Passion, aberration, bad taste, carelessness.

44. Venus to Mars
    + Pronounced need for love, sensuality, desire, artistic ability, lively expressiveness, small successes.
    - (C) Disharmonious sex life, inclination to immoderation, overexcitement, tactlessness, seduction, being unsatisfied, feeling unwell, disputes with women, pronounced eroticism.

45. Venus to Jupiter
    + (C) Sincerity, grace, warm feeling, making oneself popular, harmonious relations, sociability, pleasurable events, visits, small gifts, comfort, happiness in love, festivities.
    - Indolence, negligence, incorrect behavior, arrogance, extravagance, loss, legal conflicts.

46. Venus to Saturn
    + Sense of reality, soberness, sense of duty, thriftiness, reserve, loyalty, self-control, relations with older persons, knowing the worth of objects.
    - (C) Being unsatisfied, hardheartedness, self-torture, jealousy, sexual inhibitions, cold awakening, tendency to separation, isolation, ill health.

47. Venus to Uranus
    + Amorous excitability, sudden intensification of the senses and feelings, surprise visits, small joys.
    - (C) Sensuality, peculiarities in love life, abnormal inclinations, letting one's emotions go, moodiness, desire for independence in love, nervousness due to repressed desires, trouble.

48. Venus to Neptune
+ Respect for love on a higher plane and artistic events, a daydreaming character, enthusiasm, platonic love, many wishes, tendency for travel and great expenses.
- (C) False sense of love, bad taste, insecurity, corruptibility, impressionability, erotic aberrations, mental pain, jealousy.
49. Venus to Pluto
+ Strong feelings of love, exceptional attractiveness, intense sex life, special artistic talent, fanatic attachment.
- (C) Overpronounced sex life, lustful desire, immorality.
50. Venus to Moon's Node
+ (C) Ability to adapt, obliging, love link.
- Lack of adaptive ability, isolation, separation.
51. Venus to Ascendant
+ (C) Sincere and loving attitude toward environment, forming of acquaintanceships, social gatherings.
- Disharmonious relationship to environment.
52. Venus to Midheaven
+ Individual kind of love and affection, benevolence, love of profession, sense of beauty and art.
- Vanity, self-admiration.

Practical Examples

One elderly lady reports that she felt no effect from Venus conjunct Uranus. Soon after, she told of an unexpected visit paid her that day. She was astonished when I told her that this was the effect of the transit. Nothing out of the ordinary can be expected of such weak transits.

"Venus opposite Saturn: A day full of worry because my mother was ill due to blood poisoning." "Venus opposite Saturn at this time resulted in a slight quarrel with my mother-in-law." "Venus conjunct Uranus made me very sensually aware; I had to pull myself together." "Venus conjunct Jupiter brought me an unexpected gift. I received as a belated birthday present a lovely liqueur set."

18

Basic Interpretation----Mars

M ars, the planet of constructive and destructive energy, has
these interpretations.

Psychological Correspondence
+ Willpower, activity, courage, spirit of enterprise, joy of work and
struggle, will to action, skill.
- Violence, waste of energy, quick temper, slyness, ruthlessness.

Biological Correspondence
Muscles, sexual function. Fever (Mars transits almost always evoke
an increase of temperature during illness.), venereal disease, skin disease, accidents, injuries.

Sociological Correspondence
Fighters, bears of arms, athletes, mechanics, technicians. craftsmen,
surgeons.

Duration of Transit Influence
Two to three days.

Transits of Mars
53. Mars to Sun
+ Vigor, resoluteness, spirit of enterprise, ambition, striving for
power, desire to lead, self-assertion, recognition, success, good
business transactions and negotiation.
- (C) Rashness, impulsiveness, misuse and waste of energy, irritability, tendency to suffer accidents, danger of injury, quarrels,

increased temperature during illness, passion. If this over-impulsiveness can be kept within bounds it can be brought to good use.

54. Mars to Moon

+ Impulsiveness, passion, strong emotional excitability, attractiveness, need for love, great deal of energy and creativity, working together with women, love link, successes.

- (C) Excitable personality, unmotivated acts, inner turmoil, injury, illness or weakness due to over-expenditure of energy or vital juices. Critical for women.

55. Mars to Mercury

+ Active intellect, intellectual energy, realization of plans, spirit of enterprise, quick settlement of affairs, ambition, successful negotiations and business transactions.

- (C) Hastiness, exaggeration, nervousness, restlessness, irritability, spoiling of plans, failures, disputes, accidents or failures on trips, keen mind and sharp criticism.

56. Mars to Venus

+ Strong need for love, passion, love of social gatherings and entertainment, artistic stimulation, little successes.

- (C) Overexaggerated passion, disharmonious sex life, tactlessness, lack of self-control, being unsatisfied, oversusceptibility, disputes with women. Very strong menstrual flow.

57. Mars to Mars

+ Energy, resoluteness, activity, joy of work, aggressiveness, impulsiveness, little successes.

- (C) Wasting of energy, ruthlessness, lack of inner clam, violent acts, tendency to suffer injuries, disputes, destruction.

58. Mars to Jupiter

+ (C) Joie de vivre, linking for organization, creativity, desire to bring about positive decisions or transactions, recognition, business success, gifts, settlement of official or judicial affairs, favorable for matters of love and marriage.

- Desire to assert oneself and to bring about decisions, meeting with opposition at negotiations, conflicts, difficulties due to superiors or officials, precipitant acts.

59. Mars to Saturn

+ Willpower, concentration, power of resistance, perseverance, indefatigableness, taking work earnestly, success through unusual effort.

- (C) Severity, harshness, insubmissiveness, stubbornness, desire to overcome opposition, tendency to estrangement, separation, grief, illness.

60. Mars to Uranus
+ Intensified creativity, desire for freedom and independence, remaining undaunted, powers of quick decision, surprises.
- (C) Contradictory personality, irritation, inner turmoil, desire to release inner tension, to stand test of nerves, tendency to suffer accidents and injury, spoiling of plans, danger through machines and modern means of transportation.
61. Mars to Neptune
+ Intellectual energy, spiritualization, receptivity.
- (C) Wanting something without doing anything for it, misuse of energy, moodiness, inferiority complex, disappointments, being harmed, secret enmities, tricks behind one's back pathological states, harm through the taking of drugs, e.g. nicotine, sedatives, false medicine, inflammable fluids and gases.
62. Mars to Pluto
+ Demonstration of extraordinary energy and thereby achievement of success, fanatic working zeal.
- (C) Ruthlessness, brutality, violent acts, being harmed, danger of accidents and injury.
63. Mars to Moon's Node
+ Good cooperation, fellowship, associations, desire for offspring.
- (C) Disharmonious cooperation, disruption of associations, quarrelsomeness.
64. Mars to Ascendant
+ Imposing one's own will on others, desire to lead, working diligently with others, bringing about success.
- (C) Aggressive attitude, conflict with persons in the environment, pugilistic tendencies, quarrels, conflict.
65. Mars to Midheaven
+ power of assertion, desire to act on one's own, power of decision, consciousness of goals, vocational advantages.
- (C) Excitable personality, acting in excited state, precipitancy, aimlessness or overshooting the goal, professional conflicts.

Practical Examples

"Mars trine Jupiter brought about for me an unexpected but very advantageous professional change." "Mars trine Venus resulted in an invitation to a social gathering which turned out to be very entertaining." "Miss S. suffered a dislocated knee and is still in bed. Mars square Uranus was due." "Mars conjunct Saturn meant sudden and unexpected money worries and also a slight throat inflammation." "Mars (first house) square Moon and Mars (tenth house): I caught my apprentice red-handed at something dishonest, and this brought about very unsettling days." "Mars conjunct Neptune: My set vacation plans had to be postponed fourteen days. This was very annoying since we had invited relatives from Vienna for a visit, but who were not able to postpone their vacation to a later date." "Our child was very ill under Mars square Mercury; his head was cold as ice, his body red-hot." "Mars opposite Jupiter: I failed to have my train ticket rebate reconfirmed by my director and had to pay a fine." "Under Mars square Venus and opposite Uranus my boyfriend and I had a big talking-out with one another; my friend told me he would never come to my house again, because of all the gossip." "I was aware of the Mars influences you have described (Mars conjunct Moon opposite Saturn) and tried to find it. But on that day at 9 p.m. the effect showed through. I had to dispel a pupil who had been very impudent. It was something that had not occurred in all the ten years of my experience. I was very upset. But in awareness of the constellation, I fought against my state, so that all the other pupils had the impression of my not being moved at all by the affair."

19

Basic Interpretation----Jupiter

Jupiter is known as the planet of felicity, or harmony, of the law and of religion.

Psychological Correspondence
+ Magnanimity, liberality, generosity, constructive attitude towards things, fairness, optimism, social sense, kindness, striving for expansion and property, moral and religious endeavor.
- Unlawful attitude, extravagance, pleasure seeking, unsocial attitude, greed, materialistic attitude.

Biological Correspondence
Nutritional functions, corpulence, liver, gall bladder. Diseases of the blood, liver and lung diseases, inflammation of the diaphragm, self-poisoning, diabetes.

Sociological Correspondence
Officials, managers, men of the cloth, judges, merchants and bankers, soldiers of fortune.

Duration of Transit Influence
Three to ten days on the average, thirty days in stationary position.

Transits of Jupiter
66. Jupiter to Sun
   + (C) Good health, joie de vivre, good humor, spirit of enterprise, striving for property, social ambition, improvement of health, success in profession, successful cooperation, pleasant acquain-

tanceships, happy associations, marriage, success with authorities or superiors, good fortune in general.
- Arrogance, fastidiousness, resulting in conflict. Illness due to improper nutrition or overeating and drinking, inclination for the high life compounded with disinclination to work, failure, conflicts with the law.

67. Jupiter to Moon
+ (C) Feelings of happiness, enthusiasm, contact, readiness to help, popularity, generosity, good relations with women, friendship, love affair, social success, material advantages, foreign relations, optimistic state of mind.
- Indifference, negligence, discontent, moodiness, irritability, marital conflicts, religious or judicial conflicts, disadvantages arising from extravagance.

68. Jupiter to Mercury
+ (C) Good common sense, wealth of plans, organizational talent, optimism, success as merchant, orator, scientist, advantageous transactions, successful trip, success and recognition in tests.
- Carelessness, absentmindedness, shallowness, unreliability, tactlessness, arrogance, dishonesty, slander, speculative failure.

69. Jupiter to Venus
+ (C) Joy of love, sincerity, attractiveness, making oneself popular, receipt of affection, harmonious relations with others, living well, good sense of form, artistic success, gifts, happy friendship, engagement or marriage, good time for purchasing clothes and jewelry. Happiness and joy.
- Indolence, negligence, overaccentuated and uncontrolled emotion, inclination to excesses and extravagance, financial difficulties, illness due to overeating and drinking or other excesses, love conflicts.

70. Jupiter to Mars
+ (C) Spirit of enterprise, desire to do great things, striving for success, skill in negotiations with authorities and superiors, agreements, contracts, (engagement, marriage), will to procreation, birth.
- Opposition to regulations and authorities, tendency to exaggeration, hastiness, intemperance, being faced with a decision, conflicts, dispute, breach of contract, marital conflicts. Excessive expenditure.

71. Jupiter to Jupiter
+ No cares, content, happiness, recognition, success, living well, advantages, gifts.

- Inclination to extravagance, pleasure seeking resulting in disadvantages, discontent, bad humor, conflicts, sorrow, difficulties with authorities, reduction of credit.

72. Jupiter to Saturn
   + Calm, perseverance, patience, diligence, resolute pursuance of goal, sense of duty, responsibility, striving for possession, success in matters of real estate, feeling of well being when alone.
   - (C) Vacillation, indecision, unpleasant changes, difficulties with matters of domicile, change of co-workers, failures, trouble with the law, inclination to illness.

73. Jupiter to Uranus
   + New and fortuitous perceptions, new ideas and plans, inventions, reforms, desire to alter everything, desire to travel, happy (temporary) associations, quick comprehension of a situation; at times, profits through speculations or lottery, sudden recognition.
   - (C) Love of freedom and independence, revolutionary ideas, opposition, tactlessness, exaggeration, exceptional inner tension but which can be released ("Thank-the-Lord Constellation"), hasty acts, passing up good opportunities, philosophical, religious or political conflicts.

74. Jupiter to Neptune
   + Idealistic tendencies, receptivity to ethical and social ideas, receiving impulse from others or through change of sense, travel, far reaching plans, generosity, gaining advantage or profit without great strain, travel to faraway places.
   - Impressionability, susceptibility, daydreaming, cleft between ideal and reality, disappointments, speculative failures, being misunderstood, enmities, insults, undermining of reputation or position, political conflicts, losses; beware of confidence men and swindlers!
   C Human kindness, idealism, interest in the arts.

75. Jupiter to Pluto
   + (C) Far reaching and fanatic endeavor, pronounced desire to assert oneself, desire to be at the top, to lead, to become rich.
   - Tendency to exploit others, great failures, consequences from guilt of the past, loss of everything, loss through state, through law proceedings.

76. Jupiter to Moon's Node
   + (C) Ability to adapt, desire to enter into good relations, successful negotiations, gain of business advantages with others, partnership, engagement, marriage.
   - Disharmonious or unsocial attitude, conflicts.

77. Jupiter to Ascendant
+ (C) Picking up good connection, new acquaintanceships, good cooperation, success and recognition, creating for oneself an attractive environment or home.
- small differences, conflicts with others, opposition to ideas of others.
78. Jupiter to Midheaven
+ (C) Beginning of a harmonious and spiritual relationship, being in good humor, achievement of a new position, happy change in life, love's joy, success in life.
- Insecure relationships, changes in conditions of life and profession.

Practical Examples

Despite the fact that Jupiter has always been designated the planet of good fortune, by no means may one expect too much of its transits. Due to its relatively fast motion, Jupiter's influence will never be as strong as that of Saturn, Uranus, Neptune, or even Pluto. It is also not absolutely sure that sextiles and trines will bring about any special advantages. Rather, these are usually significant only of a harmonious state, while self-assertion is often more likely under a Jupiter square, e.g. to Mars or Sun. Some cases have demonstrated that under Jupiter opposition or square Sun or Venus, for example, especially pleasant experiences could be had, or the table was more richly beladen than usual, but where the danger existed of even greater fastidiousness or of illness through some nutritional error. However, those who are well in control of themselves, will gain more under square and opposition than under trine and sextiles. Here, some extracts from correspondence:

"Jupiter in Taurus trine Mercury brought me small gifts, for example, a little Mignon-Typewriter, which I only have to do a little repair work on." "Jupiter over Mercury brought me two professional successes." "Under Jupiter sextile Venus Mr. M. met a young widow, a millionairess, at a ball. They will be getting married soon." "After a long period of uncertainty I finally received a patent on my invention at the beginning of February under Jupiter sextile Jupiter. At this time, I was happier than usual. Suddenly, I comprehended many a problem and riddle of life, the meaning and actual point of living." "Jupiter trine Mercury was due on April 1; at this time I obtained approval from the post office director for my transfer to Z.; it became effective on May 1, under Jupiter trine Venus."

"Jupiter square Neptune: Just as I received your letter and was reading about this constellation, a pupil and her mother came to pay a bill, whereby she deducted, without a by-your-leave, 5 RM. It is peculiar that such people can never stop thinking of their own profit and gain. I was so very indignant at his impertinence that I felt like throwing her out. I can become very much angered when an honest person cannot assert his rights and the swindler is triumphant."

"Jupiter conjunct Sun: optimism, improvement in living conditions, periodic good and unusually luxurious living." "Jupiter conjunct Ascendant: receipt of a valuable gift from a lady, gain from acquaintanceship with a woman. Visit with mother with ensuing advantages, receipt of many groceries." "Jupiter opposite Ascendant trine Venus: the principal month of the whole year, success in legal disputes, making peace with the neighbors, marriage, fulfillment of hopes and dreams, move to home of own. Receipt of large remittance and a parcel of valuable books."

20

Basic Interpretation----Saturn

Saturn is the executer of fate, leading man onward through his various experiences, but which also can inhibit him and render him incapable.

Psychological Correspondence
+ Powers of concentration, steadiness, constancy, earnestness, profundity, thriftiness.
- Inhibition, melancholy, taciturnity, loneliness, isolation, separation, fear, mistrust, envy, stinginess, avarice, lack of adaptive ability.

Biological Correspondence
Frame, skin, spleen. Mental disorders, paralyses, lingering and slow-healing illness, leprosy, blood impurities, colds.

Sociological Correspondence
Hardworking, inhibited and melancholy persons, elderly persons, father, farmers, miners, property owners.

Duration of Transit influence
Eight to fourteen days; up to eight weeks in stationary position.

Transits of Saturn
79. Saturn to Sun
+ Perseverance, powers of concentration, indefatigability, self-assertion, improvement of health, recognition for diligence, support through older persons, simple life.

- (C) Reduced mental faculties and physical development, pessimistic attitude, mental suffering, illness, estrangement, separation, grief, family, troubles, professional difficulties.

80. Saturn to Moon
+ Inner calm, content, self-control, circumspection, sense of duty, success through diligence and activity, good relations with older women, sincere relationships, desire to travel.
- (C) Inhibitions, fluctuating moods, inferiority complex, melancholy, obstinacy, unstableness of character, illness (due to mental suffering), lack of self-confidence, fear of exposure, difficulties ensuing from change or travel, estrangement, separation (possibly through death).

81. Saturn to Mercury
+ Powers of concentration, careful thinking, diligence, logical thinking, objectivity, love of order and thoroughness, patience, success in scientific work, long trips, business enterprises.
- (C) Mental and spiritual backwardness, occupational difficulties, tedious work, estrangement, separation, disadvantageous news, tendency to illness (especially in respect to head and nerves, and according to disposition, also inclination to speech defects and hearing disorders).

82. Saturn to Venus
+ Sense of reality, soberness, sense of duty, faithfulness, self-control, earnestness and sincerity, relationships with mature women, genuine artistic activity.
- (C) Discontent, hard-heartedness, disillusionment, isolation, estrangement, conflicts arising from jealousy, separation, having to make sacrifices, financial difficulties, immoral acts, inclination to illness, disappointment in matters of love.

83. Saturn to Mars
+ Perseverance, power of resistance, indefatigability in overcoming difficulties.
- (C) Dissatisfaction or displeasure stemming from great difficulties and antagonisms, severity, harshness, insubmissiveness, weakness, inclination to illness, danger of injuries or mishaps, mental and emotional pain, sorrow, harm from others.

84. Saturn to Jupiter
+ Achievement of goals through perseverance, earnest endeavors, tendency to changes in residence, persistent pursuance of aims, success in negotiations with superiors or authorities, favorable settlement of legal disputes, self-confidence, philosophic thinking, desire for possessions, separations seen in a favorable light,

feeling of well-being when alone.

- (C) Dissatisfaction with one's self and others, quick irritability, indecisiveness, opposition and protest, conflicts, lack of self-confidence, pessimism, inclination to illness, occupational difficulties owing to financial worries.

85. Saturn to Saturn
+ Patience, perseverance, powers of concentration, success through effort and industry, earnest endeavors.
- (C) Developmental crisis mentally or in terms of health, beginning of new phase of life, illness, depression, displeasure, inefficiency, sorrow.

86. Saturn to Uranus
+ Calm and collected thinking, methodic carrying out of new undertakings or changes, powers of perseverance, mastering of every situation, success in technical affairs or with inventions, extensive travel.
- (C) Use of force or suffering of violence, nonsubmission, struggle for existence, backlash from past mistakes, disputes, resistance, losses, mental and emotional pain, sudden estrangement or separation, sorrow, danger of accidents, mishaps, or machine damage.

87. Saturn to Neptune
+ Engrossment in difficult problems, unusual spiritual experiences, interest in the occult, out of the ordinary acquaintanceships, longing for faraway places, travel.
- (C) Agonizing mental and emotional inhibitions, enervating circumstances, illness (neuroses) whose causes are difficult to find, troubles in public, in occupation or the family, secret enmities, deception, danger or infection (poisoning), sorrow, loss, making sacrifices.

88. Saturn to Pluto
+ Working hard to achieve success, participation in mass efforts, inclination more towards action than to words, fanatic and toiling endeavor,
- (C) Being cheated of success from work done, loss through force majeure, suffering from violence or committing violent acts (murder).

89. Saturn to Moon's Node
+ Connection or cooperation with older or experienced persons,
- (C) Feeling of being repressed by others, estrangement, inhibitions, separation (bereavement), disadvantage or loss due to others, mutual sorrow.

90. Saturn to Ascendant

+ Perseverance, ability to overcome many difficulties, gaining of experience, being together with older persons.
- (C) Depressed surroundings, sharing sorrow with others, bereavement, estrangement, separation, living in straightened or impoverished circumstances, illness, hospital stay.

91. Saturn to Midheaven
+ Clinging to hopes, gaining of experience, change of aim and its untiring pursuance, ability to persevere.
- (C) Checks in development, necessity to fight against difficulties, estrangement, separation, sorrow, mental suffering through mother or wife, mourning of these persons.

Practical Examples

The transits of Saturn over its own radical position, or in opposition or square to this position, usually correspond to developmental crises signifying the end of one phase and the beginning of a new one, which in the main has a duration of roughly seven years. Those who look back upon their lives will usually be able to ascertain several such seven year periods, which, however, do not necessarily have to be connected with Saturn transits over the radical position, but rather can be connected with Saturn transits over the solar position or over planet clusters in one sign as well. Saturn transits can only then be termed critical when Saturn is moving very slowly or is stationary and makes a mutual appearance with other critical constellations. Therefore, the tendency to give every Saturn transit a fateful interpretation is completely unfounded; many Saturn transits are harmless.

Below are some examples from reports sent to us:

"I have had various experiences with Saturn transits, Saturn conjunct Sun, Mercury square Moon: my last and not very happy year of childhood filled with trouble and worries about vocation, my childish joy destroyed. Saturn conjunct Venus: separation from loved ones. Saturn conjunct Moon square Sun, Mercury: death of both grandparents, much sadness, unpleasant and bleak home with mother, difficulties, dependency, poverty, depression. Saturn square Moon, Moon's Node opposite Sun, Mercury: unsuccessful attempts at getting ahead, uncertain circumstances, deceit and loss of money through partners in business, difficulties away from home. Saturn square Saturn: futile efforts, many obstacles, useless work, lack of income. Saturn conjunct Mars and Midheaven opposite Jupiter: deterioration and subsequent destruction of my own home life, despondent and lonely member of household, taking over of great obligations. After surviving the hard times, creation of my own respectable home." "Due on the day of dear mother's death were: Saturn conjunct Moon and Sun opposite Sun."

"Saturn square Sun (in tenth) brought unemployment of husband, family worries and illness." "During the day I was very upset and nervous under Saturn conjunct jupiter, and in the evening I got into an argument with my boss where I gave notice. Through mediation, my giving notice could be revoked. However, the repetition of this constellation had again as a consequence giving of notice and serious conflicts."

21

Basic Interpretation----Uranus

U ranus represents a concentrated power which can make its
appearance suddenly and intensely.

Psychological Correspondence
+ Originality, love of freedom, self-will, sense of rhythm, intuition.
- Extravagant behavior, inconsistency, revolutionary character, con-
trariness, erratic character.

Biological Correspondence
Nervous system, the meninges, pituitary gland, spinal marrow, nerve
and cerebral disorders, injuries, operations, accidents.

Sociological Correspondence
Reformers, inventors, technicians, anarchists, revolutionaries.

Duration of Transit Influence
Two to ten weeks depending on orbiting or stationary condition.

Transits of Uranus
92. Uranus to Sun
+ Originality, foresight, organizational flair, tendency to sudden
changes, alteration and travel, improvement of life position, bet-
terment of health through new methods of treatment, sudden
recognition, professional advancement, in the case of women,
often a sudden involvement with a man.
- (C) Sudden urge or compulsion to change, critical effects, sudden
disposition to illness, in the case of illness possibility of surgery,

times of upset or crisis in partnership or marriage, upset through influence of male persons.

93. Uranus to Moon
+ Intensified intellectual stimulation, wealth of plans, urge to change, alteration, travel, sudden acquaintanceship with female persons, sudden love-links, but which are seldom of long duration, special scientific knowledge, inventions.
- (C) Sudden mental and emotional upsets, lack of inner calm, nervousness, tendency towards extravagance, confusion of feelings and thoughts, impractical ideas, sudden failures, upsets in matters of love or marriage, births, danger in surgical operations.

94. Uranus to Mercury
+ Inventive spirit, desire for change of pace or alteration, organizational talent, good intuition, good critical faculty, invention, new plans and stimuli, intellectual flexibility, new connections, sudden journeys. Interest in cosmobiology.
- (C) Wasting one's energy, nervous haste, errors, mistakes, moodiness, obstinacy failures, upsetting of plans, upsets through letters or gossip, nervous disorder (in rare cases, thoughts of suicide).

95. Uranus to Venus
+ Great excitability in love-life, sudden intensification of emotional feelings, sudden and strong attraction (but rarely of any duration), new acquaintanceships, new stimuli for artistic work, sense of form and rhythm, creativity, (with impulsive persons) tendency to amorous adventures and infidelity.
- (C) Egotistical attitude to love, inclination to perversity, tendency to be guided by emotion, hypersensitivity, moodiness, nervousness owing to suppressed desires, pronounced sexual motivation, aberration, discontent because of excess, danger of sexual assault.

96. Uranus to Mars
+ Extraordinary energy, desire for freedom and independence, non-submissiveness, technical skill, tendency to hastiness.
- (C) Restlessness, nervousness, obstinacy, stubbornness, brutality, intolerance, danger of accident, injury, or separation, harm through machines, fire, explosion, turbulent change in life, placed under compulsion, mistakes due to haste. If possible, avoid travel!

97. Uranus to Jupiter
+ Ideas, inventions, striving for knowledge, good at negotiating, changes, organizational matters, sudden and advantageous connections with prominent persons, sudden recognition or success.
- (C) Love of freedom, desire for independence, opposition, non-submission, insistence on one's own principles purely for the sake

of opposition, tactlessness, lack of adaptability, conflicts, in marriage as well, legal disputes, great psychological tensions and upsets leading to sudden changes.

98. Uranus to Saturn

+ Being in control of every situation, strong resistance, perseverance, indefatigability, success in coping with demands of life, occupational changes, change of residence.

- (C) Great psychological tension, inflexibility, provoking behavior, contradiction, dispute, animosity, estrangement, separation, bereavement, illness, hardships, formative interference in destiny (prison).

99. Uranus to Uranus

+ Spirit of enterprise, creativity, change in life after period of crisis, multitude of plans, tendency to reform and change, end of one and beginning of another phase of life.

- (C) Hard conditions of life which are usually followed by change, danger of catastrophes, nervous crisis (thoughts of suicide).

100. Uranus to Neptune

+ Peculiar emotional states, impressionable and receptive, inspiration, spiritual perception, interest in religious and spiritual, and mystical problems, longing for faraway places, travel, inclination to delve into the occult.

- (C) Inner tension and obscurity lead to the forming of extreme goals, instability, mental and emotional conflict, deplorable conditions, harm from others due to lack of resistance, undermining of reputation, losses, illness (including danger of poisoning).

101. Uranus to Pluto

+ Indefatigability, untiring resolve, struggle for reform and innovation, fanatic striving for transformation, strong sense of goals, creation of new conditions of life.

- (C) Life crisis, suffering under acts of violence or force majeure, heavy losses, being placed in a serious dilemma, great agitation, involvement in mass catastrophes.

102. Uranus to Moon's Node

+ Joint experiences with others, sudden acquaintanceships and connections possibly resulting in a change of situation.

- (C) Unexpected incidents in community or family life, unsettling experiences with others, mourning with others.

103. Uranus to Ascendant

+ Quick reaction to environmental influences, sudden acquaintanceships, transformation of environment, moving to another place.

- (C) Unsettling experiences with others, danger of accident or injury, unexpected incidents, sudden threat, bereavement.
104. Uranus to MC
    + Determination, bringing about changes, change of profession, rapid progress, change of residence,
    - (C) Hastiness, incidents, turning points of destiny, isolation from others, vacillation in aims of life, decisive events.

Practical Examples

Uranus is the great instigator of change, and whose course through the zodiac corresponds to certain periods of life. Every seven years or so, Uranus changes signs; at twenty-two years, it enters square and at twenty-eight years trine to its radical position, and thus corresponds in the main to the decisive events in life. At forty-two to forty-five years, Uranus in opposition to the radical position represents the high point of life with its various crises and the beginning of the decline. Therefore, the Uranus constellation need not always evoke extraordinary events, but rather can reflect the inner development manifested in a lifetime.

A few reports: "One lady acquaintance tells of a sexual assault under Uranus square Moon, also due were: Moon opposite Mars sextile Jupiter, Neptune square Ascendant, Mars square Moon, Venus sextile Mercury." "As you very correctly mentioned, the square of Uranus to Neptune brought me into difficulties with the management of where I work, which, in order to humiliate me, I suppose, approached me in a very ill-bred manner."

"On Saturday an acquaintance of mine, a very kindhearted man, suddenly shot himself in the train. On the previous evening, I had gone for a walk with him until 11 p.m. He gave no sign of anything wrong or of what he intended to do. The reason for his suicide was a court decision lost in a matter of alimony and poor earnings. The suicide had in his radical chart Neptune in the eighth house in opposition to Uranus, which does indicate this kind of death (but not always, only in special cases! R.E.). In addition, Uranus square Uranus were due on the day of his death: Sun conjunct Ascendant, Moon square Sun, Mars, Neptune opposite Sun, Mars conjunct Venus, Jupiter square Mercury."

"Uranus (Pisces) opposite Venus (Virgo) gave me a bad reputation; I had an accident, inflammation of the ankle joint, and pain in the intestines." "Uranus opposite Mars leads to animosity, conflict and upset." "Uranus square Saturn was manifest on the due date through fever, shivering and weakness, and also through fainting. The examination on the following day showed irritation of the appendix, gall bladder, liver and kidneys, nervous strain, stomach and intestinal disorder."

22

Basic Interpretation----Neptune

Neptune is the mysterious, the unfathomable planet. It greatly influences our spiritual life, in the positive and in the negative sense.

Psychological Correspondence
+ Receptivity, sensibility, inspiration contemplativeness, empathy, tendency to mysticism, all-encompassing love.
- Impressionability, hypersensitivity, obscurity, confusion, deception, aimlessness, lies, deceit.

Biological Correspondence
Pineal glad, solar plexus, aura. Illnesses difficult in their diagnosis and often psychosomatic, mental disease, poisoning, infections, paralyses.

Sociological Correspondence
Those with negative attitude, impressionable persons, mediums, dubious persons, tricksters, practitioners of slight-of-hand, but also prominent, spiritually oriented personalities.

Duration of Transits Influence
Four to eight weeks; in stationary positions up to three months; frequent repetition of the same aspects within two years' time.

Transits of Neptune
105. Neptune to Sun
+ Receptivity for all impressions, inspiration, enthusiasm, inclina-

tion to mysticism and profundity, stimulation of intellectual work, intellectual and spiritual experience, peace of mind, companionship of souls.
- (C) Impressionability, negative character, tendency to alcohol and nicotine, etc., physical weakness and susceptibility for illnesses, lack of determination, confusion in mental processes, unpleasant dreams, self-delusion, damage to reputation, disappointment through others, undermining of relationships, caution when taking toxic medications which may only be administered in small doses.

106. Neptune to Moon
+ Sensitivity, empathy, introspection, far-ranging wishes, active dream life, longing for faraway places, extensive travel, plans for change, spiritual relationships with women.
- (C) Illusions, disappointments, instability, being misunderstood, danger from occult experiences, disappointment in friendship or marriage, extravagances, dissipation, danger of infection, trouble in public life or in profession, mental suffering.

107. Neptune to Mercury
+ Imagination, rich fantasy, intuitive thinking, perception of the most intricate and profound interrelations, creativity, stimulating exchange of ideas, acquaintanceship with those of the same way of thinking, extensive travel.
- (C) False thinking, poor judgment, confused ideas, hypersensitivity, overactive fantasy, insincerity, inclination to lies and pretense, uncontrolled emotional life, nervous disorders, undermining of reputation, defamation, danger of swindle. Caution with contracts and documents!

108. Neptune to Venus
+ Sensitivity in love life, devotion, impressionability. Sense of beauty and art, good taste, profound relationship to loved ones, stimulation of artistic activity, pleasurable travels, interest in poetry and the romantic.
- (C) False feelings of love, bad taste, susceptibility, erotic aberration, eccentric habits, danger of infection, illness due to excess, disappointment in love, renunciation, jealousy.

109. Neptune to Mars
+ Desire to fulfill wishes and realize plans, urge to travel far, intellectual perception, receiving and giving stimulation, receiving good advice. Disappointment will often be experienced because of ventures into fields removed from reality, leaving the practicalities of life aside.
- (C) Wishes not followed up by action, inability to develop energy,

misuse of energy, inclination to take sedatives, or alcohol, nicotine, etc., moodiness, physical weakness and susceptibility for illness, disappointments, deceit, disagreeable matters, criminal occurrences. Initiative and working energy are paralyzed.

110. Neptune to Jupiter

+ Hopefulness, trust in the future, high ideals, spiritual and intellectual relations, social understanding, generosity, favorable disposition, extensive and pleasurable travel, recognition and success, acquaintanceship with prominent personalities, at times profits or advantages without any effort on one's own part.

- (C) False hopes, disposition toward illegal acts, injudicious speculation, susceptibility, losses, disadvantages from political affairs, damage to reputation, undermining of relationships through deceit, defamation, harassed legal situation. Pecuniary loss through extortioners, swindlers, and confidence men.

111. Neptune to Saturn

+ Gaining of experience, engrossment, getting ahead gradually by effort and perseverance, working methodically.

- (C) Suffering, sacrifice, being in conflict with one's own self, feeling of insecurity, going through enervating circumstances, tendency to illness especially nervous disorders with psychosomatic causes, difficulties, inhibitions, separation, sorrow.

112. Neptune to Uranus

+ Interest in intellectual problems, new problems, new ideas and views, peculiar mental states, inspiration, broadening of points of view, travel. Foreign relations, turning points of life, relationship to the occult.

- (C) Impressionability, lack of resistance and energy, confused mental and emotional state, eccentric inclinations, unconscious actions, difficult circumstances, professional disadvantages, concealed attacks, undermining of good reputation, chaotic relations, illness due to infection or poisoning, heavy losses, catastrophe. (These latter effects only come about when they are indicated by other constellations.)

113. Neptune to Neptune

+ Period of spiritual development, intellectual perception, travel.

- (Conjunction not possible!) Change in life, life crisis in consequence of disappointment or illness.

114. Neptune to Pluto

+ Coping with unusual problems, unusual interests and endeavors, spiritual orientation, far-ranging connections, extensive travel.

- (C) Peculiar mental states, possessed by fantastic ideas, collapse of an idea, self-torture, heavy losses, strange illness.

115. Neptune to Moon's Node
+ Expecting much of a relationship, joining a peculiar or mystical community.
- (C) Expecting too much or the wrong thing of an association or community leading to mutual disappointment, experiencing joint disappointments, lack of fellowship, damage suffered because of being member of a community.

116. Neptune to Ascendant
+ Susceptibility to environmental influence, entering into peculiar associations, intellectual affinity with others, indulgement of certain illusions.
- (C) Depression due to others, disappointment through others, breach of trust, falseness, deceit, dealings with swindlers or calumniators, illness stemming from mental suffering.

117. Neptune to Midheaven
+ Devotion to peculiar aims, resorting to pretence or having to play a role, many ideas or plans without realization.
- (C) Pursuance of false ideas, self-delusion, failures, losses, professional disadvantages, losses due to deceit or false friends.

Practical Examples

Neptune transits are most usually connected with the intensification of imagination and the formation of ideas and plans and also lead to daydreaming, and hence to loss of sense of reality. Therefore, in its negative effects, Neptune can bring about false ideas, confusion and illusions which are particularly detrimental to mental and emotional stability, and indeed, can possibly lead to psychoses. Extraordinary events are not always the result of Neptune transits, but rather these constellations reflect exalted or depressed emotional states. The following were featured in a female horoscope:

Neptune conjunct Moon square Sun, Mercury: Time of confusion, misunderstandings, errors, failure in all endeavors, self-delusion, self-torture, poor social conditions, in the company of unstable or rootless persons, insecure financial circumstances, loss of reputation, loss through theft, estrangement from parents, stay in hospital.

Neptune conjunct Moon, trine Saturn: help through older persons, engrossment in mystical or religious problems, extensive spiritual development, travel books based on own experiences. Neptune trine Sun and Mercury: serene or stable conditions, activity in seclusion, reading and study. Neptune square Saturn: loss of income, straightened circumstances, difficulties, failure, time of desolation due to rival in love and the dissolution of a love relationship, secret rival, slander, mental suffering, illness due to nutritional poisoning and overenjoyment. "For weeks, I felt the trine of Neptune to Venus to be very beneficial, just as if a warm and friendly light had spread itself over everything and had bound me with everything under the Sun. As the transit became exact, I met many people connected with the anthroposiphical movement; it was a very strange and peculiar meting."

"I feel the effect of Neptune especially strong since it brings to mind very unpleasant things, things that one has done without thinking and which cannot be undone. This is when Neptune tries to tempt me into making backhanded attacks, e.g. to denounce someone, to write anonymous letters or make anonymous reports on someone. Through willpower, I have always been able to suppress such disgusting and mean urges, and on the other hand I receive the good emanations all the more strongly."

The following report was made about Neptune square Mars and Uranus conjunct Neptune: "I had told my sister and nurses of your letter and asked them by no means to give an injection during the critical weeks. I myself only found this out three days later. However, my sister wrote these lines at the conclusion of her report: 'After Mother had told me of the change in blood it occurred to me that we shouldn't give any injection because of possible blood poisoning. Now it has all come about, just as you were told by Mr. E.; since her injection, Mother has been feeling worse from day to day.'" Of significance in this case is that there was a New Moon on the day of the injection. "As Uranus conjunct Neptune became exact, death came after another morphine injection had been given."

23

Basic Interpretation----Pluto

Pluto was the last planet to be discovered. Even though there have been many examples of Plutonian influence during the past years, general experience is still relatively small. The catchwords for Pluto, power and mass, have proven on the whole to be applicable, as the practical examples will show.

Psychological Correspondence
+ Desire for power, ruthless frankness, striving for influence over the masses, propagandistic efforts, sympathy with the masses.
- Ruthless use of force, fanatic proselytism, agitating efforts, narrow-mindedness.

Biological Correspondence
The subconscious.

Sociological Correspondence
Persons who have hypnotic influence over the masses, such as propagandists, orators, actors, and politicians of definite and one-sided opinion.

Duration of Transit Influence
Several months. Influence usually shows up suddenly and with a very lasting effect.

Transits of Pluto
118. Pluto to Sun
+ Striving for power through physical strength or mental effort,

unusual creative energy, concentration on goals, self-assertion, taking command, realization of new ideas.

- (C) Disadvantages due to overambition or arrogance, exposure to great danger, physical suffering, martyrdom, lingering illness (heart trouble), separation from a man, marriage dissolved through superior force.

119. Pluto to Moon

+ Rich but one-sided emotional life, great emotional excitability, ruthless pursuit of goals.

- (C) Strong outbursts of feeling, e.g. jealousy, wounded vanity, insult to honor, etc., emotional shock, unusual disease, separation, grief.

120. Pluto to Mercury

+ Desire for public acclamation, professional ambition, success as orator, writer, advertising executive, unceasing pursuit or aim.

- (C) Overestimation of capabilities and overeagerness leading to nervous disorders, propensity for swindle, professional crisis.

121. Pluto to Venus

+ Exceptional power of attraction, intense need for love, active sexual life, "madly in love" with partner, strong feeling of attraction to a person as if under inner compulsion, artistic creativity.

- (C) Overaccentuated sex life, sensual desires, tensions in love life, immorality, adultery.

122. Pluto to Mars

+ Show of unusual energy, great self-confidence, working fever, ambition, achievement of great success.

- (C) Use of brutal means, disregard of others, to have to suffer violence, accidents with long lasting consequences.

123. Pluto to Jupiter

+ Desire for great influence in spiritual or material fields, desire to lead the masses, to bring about social or religious reform, brilliant organizational talent, achievement of great success, attainment of wealth.

- (C) Pursuit of fanatic goals, desire to exploit others, extravagance, loss of everything, conflict with authorities, arrest.

124. Pluto to Saturn

+ Advance through tenacity, perseverance and untiring effort, self-discipline, sacrifice, participation in public efforts, to be silent and act.

- (C) Severity, violent acts, fanatic vandalism, suffering under hard-heartedness or brutality, to be cheated of hard work's success. (In rare cases, death, murder.)

125. Pluto to Uranus
   + Indefatigable work, achievement through immense effort, carrying out of innovations or changes, building anew, setting up of a new life.
   - Violence, excitement, subversive plans, confrontation with the question of "either-or," difficult decisions, unforeseen and vitally important crisis, sudden separation, death.

126. Pluto to Neptune
   + Refined spiritual life, great sensitivity, active imagination, subject to illusion, unusual experiences, transcendental inclinations, spirituality.
   - (C) Obscurity in inner life, peculiar circumstances, pursuit of fantastic ideas with subsequent disappointment, self-torture, craving for alcohol, nicotine, caffeine, etc., possessed with an idea, severe loss, danger through forces of nature.

127. Pluto to Pluto
   + and - hardly ever occur due to Pluto's slowness; no experience has been gathered as yet.

128. Pluto to Moon's Node
   + Personal connections have decisive influence on fate, contact and common experience with many persons, mass gatherings.
   - (C) Sharing of tragic fate in common with others, separation through superior force, grief.

129. Pluto to Ascendant
   + Desire to rule over those in environment, getting one's own way, coming into an unaccustomed situation, including new acquaintances and associations.
   - (C) Fateful disputes, mishap, injury, separation, forceful change of residence, arrest.

130. Pluto to Midheaven:
   + Urge for recognition, power of self-assertion, to feel called upon to function as organizer or leader, to obtain recognition, desire to plan one's own future life, to seek professional acknowledgement, attainment of a position of power.
   - (C) Foolhardiness, licentiousness, abuse of power, triggering or experiencing resistance and revenge, professional crisis, fall from the top.

Practical Examples

Experience has shown that the transits of Pluto do not need always exercise an influence; they often pass over without a trace. They do play an important role, however, when an individual is involved in some mass fate, for example, war, air raids, concentration camps, or mass escapes.

Under Sun square Pluto separation from spouse through superior force has often been noted, for example, through imprisonment or consequences of war. Pluto over Neptune in Leo brought about a heart ailment lasting many years, as long as Pluto remained in this position. Under Pluto conjunct Mars a man was buried alive and as a consequence lost his memory to the extent that he could not even remember his own name over a long period of time. Under Pluto square or opposite Jupiter, several persons were arrested, came into conflict with the authorities, or lost job and fortune.

In one case, Pluto over Saturn brought about violent death; in another case, total loss of fortune. Pluto conjunct Neptune in one case gave cause to forebodings, and in another, to emotional confusion. Pluto over the Ascendant had as a consequence loss of job and change of life. Pluto over the Midheaven led to great losses. Pluto opposite the Ascendant caused complete change of life including suffering due to stepmother and leaving home.

Pluto opposite Jupiter led to serious disputes within the family. Under Pluto trine the Midheaven, one young man took his fate into his own hands and went his way to build up a new existence under his own power. Pluto opposite Moon reuslted in separation and breaking up of a relationship, and as this position was due again, another relationship failed. Pluto square the Midheaven brought about a complete change of vocation after a period of uncertainty and insecurity.

24

Basic Interpretation----Moon's Node

The Moon's Node is not the designation for a celestial body, but rather, it is the intersecting point of the lunar orbit with the ecliptic. A differentiation is made between an ascending ☊ (Dragon's Head) and a descending ☋ (Dragon's Tail) Lunar Node.

For the purposes of simplification, the ascending Moon's Node will be under discussion here, the descending Node always being directly opposite in the zodiac. Only the ascending Node is given in the ephemerides. The Moon's Node is indicative of "knots and ties," meetings. Up to now, these transits had hardly been given notice in textbooks. The following compilation, therefore, represents an entirely new study.

Psychological Correspondence
+ Ability to adapt, seeking of relationships, sociability, fellowship, friendly personality.
- Lack of adaptive ability, unsociability, unsocial behavior, incompatibility.

Sociological Correspondence
Gatherings, associations, contacts, mediators, blood relationships, relatives.

Durations of Transit Influence
Two to three weeks.

Transits of the Ascending Moon's Node
131. Moon's Node to Sun

+ (C) Spiritual or physical relationships, relationship with spouse, public affairs.
- Breaking off of relationships, estrangement from male persons, separation.

132. Moon's Node to Moon
(C) Spiritual attitude in relationships with others, relationship with women or migratory folk.
- Lack of adaptive ability, breaking off of relations with women.

133. Moon's Node to Mercury
+ (C) Liking for exchange of ideas with others, social or business ties.
- Unpopularity, breaking off of relations, retirement of partner or fellow worker.

134. Moon's Node to Venus
+ (C) Adaptable, obliging, attractive personality, object of affection, love link, engagement, spiritual relationship, artistic connections.
- Disharmonious love relationship, estrangement, separation, unpleasant personality.

135. Moon's Node to Mars
+ Cooperation, sexual relationship, fellowship, desire of children, joint successes.
- (C) Destruction of collaboration, upset in household, estrangement through dispute.

136. Moon's Node to Jupiter
+ (C) Harmonious relationship to others, joyful experience shared with others, happiness as couple, gaining of a good partner, engagement or marriage.
- Disharmonious or unsocial behavior in relationships, conflicts.

137. Moon's Node to Saturn
+ Relationships with older persons or protection through them, earnest cooperation.
- (C) Obstacles and difficulties in relationships, isolation of self or separation, disadvantages or loss through others, dissolution of blood relations, bereavement.

138. Moon's Node to Uranus
+ Sudden relations and acquaintanceships, common experience with others, temporary acquaintanceships.
- (C) Sudden incidents in communal life, upsets with others, conflicts.

139. Moon's Node to Neptune
+ Great expectations from a cooperative effort, placing of hopes in others, spiritual contact, secret relationships.

- (C) Lack of community sense, delusions about relations with others, self-disappointment, separation due to intrigues.
140. Moon's Node to Pluto
   + Relationships, possibility with fateful turn.
   - (C) Common and severe fate, estrangement, separation.
141. Moon's Node to Moon's Node
   + (C) Possibilities for connections or approach.
   - Estrangement, also bereavement.
142. Moon's Node to Ascendant
   + (C) Good relation to environment, pleasant collaboration, acquaintanceships, relationships.
   - A life together made difficult, estrangement, separation, grief.
143. Moon's Node to Midheaven
   + (C) Personal ties, coming together with those of the same mind and common endeavors, forming an association to pursue common aims, spiritual relationships, friendship, engagement, marriage.
   - Difficulties in joint endeavors, professional difficulties, withdrawal from an association.

Practical Examples

"Moon's Node trine Saturn brought me protection through an elderly gentleman." "Moon's Node trine Jupiter made possible for me a particularly joyful Christmas in the company of others." "Under Moon's Node trine Moon I met my future wife at a convention." "It was possible under Moon's Node conjunct Sun again to start publishing a newspaper after a half-year's injunction, and thereby again be active in the public light."

"Moon's Node square Saturn corresponded to my separation from the family when inducted." "Moon's Node square Neptune brought me in the company of criminals during protective custody." "Moon's Node opposite Mercury corresponded to difficulties in working with others in my profession as well as in the household." "Under Moon's Node conjunct Mars trine Jupiter I finally succeeded in getting a decision on my attaining a very lovely apartment. At the same time I could let my family know they could immediately set off for the new city of residence."

"Under Moon's Node opposite Saturn I was temporarily separated from my family due to circumstances beyond my control." "You wrote me that Saturn in conjunction with the ascending Lunar Node could bring about a death. This has now come to pass. My dear mother has just passed away." "Moon's Node trine Venus brought me a new and advantageous acquaintanceship and enlivened business activity for me.''

"A few days after receiving the chart from you would be the time when he should experience his fatal car accident. This upset me greatly, since I was unable to warn him. At the hour of the mishap, Moon transited the point for illness and death on the cusp of the eighth house. Simultaneously, Uranus reached the Moon's Node. This is most probably the position which brought him death.''

25

Appendix

The current edition of this book is pretty much the same as the edition of 1952. This fulfills the wish of the many readers of this popular book. It is necessary, however, to discuss certain problems in detail and to supplement the work done in the past in order to come up to the present standard of cosmobiological research.

As already stated in Chapter 2, Aspects in the Cosmogram, the angles (aspects) of the stellar bodies are of greater importance than the signs and houses. The author has in the meanwhile completely discarded any interpretation based on the houses, or better yet, fields, and now only applies those points consistent in every system of houses, namely the medium coeli (Midheaven) and the Ascendant. Other authors on the subject now have also rejected the traditional interpretations according to houses. The various sytems of houses have among themselves deviations so great that in one case a planet will be a particular house according to the one system, but in an entirely different house according to the other system. This results in uncertainty which can only lead to error in interpretation. The author has traced the origin of the division of houses. The problem is treated extensively in the author's pamphlet "Hermes Trimegistos, Die Lehre der 12 Häuser."

The orbs of the aspects have today been much reduced. The following rule has been set up:

The orb amounts to a maximum five degrees
with the personal points (Midheaven, Ascen-

dant, Sun, Moon), to a maximum four degrees with the fast moving planets (Mercury, Venus, Mars), to a maximum three degrees with the slow moving planets (Jupiter, Saturn, Uranus, Neptune, Pluto) and the ascending Moon's Node.

According to this rule, the individual importance increases with the rate of speed. Whole generations are encompassed in the positions of the slow moving planets, whereas the positions of the fast moving planets relate to the same birth dates within a year, and the individual points to day, hour, minute.

An important factor in the interpretation of the transits is that those aspects are significant which result from the progressive division of the circle, i.e. conjunction-opposition (bisection), square and semisquare or sesquiquadrate (division of the circle by eighths). One can generally assume that when transits form such aspects, something is "happening," whereas, as the author wrote 40 years previously the sextiles and trines are more expressive of a state or condition: an individual is healthy, happy, or discontent and in bad humor. Therefore, especially the hard angles derived from the progressive division of the circle come into consideration for a prognostication. The semisquares and the sesquiquadrates should not be neglected since their importance has been variously proven by statistics.

According to the international nomenclature, instead of the abbreviation "p" for progressing, "t" for transiting may also be used. Accordingly, Sun-t-0-Jupiter means that transiting Sun is in conjunction with Jupiter, or Mars-90-Uranus designates a square of Mars to Uranus. This method of writing is of advantage in that it can also be written on word processing equipment.

Nowadays we no longer write the aspect points in the outer margin of the cosmogram, since it is possible using the forty-five degree ephemerides to gain within a few minutes' time a quick overall view of the year's most important transits. This method of work will be explained a bit later on.

This would also make the setting up of a table of transits, as shown on page sixteen, superfluous. Here, we might add, the effect of a transit is usually already past by the time it is actually due. The due date, therefore, cannot be taken to determine the middle, but rather the end point of the effect. This fact becomes especially apparent in the examination of the yearly diagrams with the graphic ephemerides. The rule set up by the author to the effect that a transit is influential only for the time it takes the progressing star to move one degree of the zodiac, has time and time again been borne out. The important thing to remember is that the falling due means practically the end of the effect.

In past decades, the parallels have been neglected because the expected influence could be ascertained.

For many readers, the evaluation of the transits presents a particular problem. The table on page twenty-eight provides some help, but for the correct evaluation, the "cosmic state" of a stellar body is always conclusive. This state is apparent when the half-sums are also considered and a structural picture of the cosmogram is set up. Since this method cannot be explained in a few words, please refer to the author's book *Mensch im All.*

In Chapter 10, The Interpretion of the Monthly Prognostication, reference is made to an evaluation according to the position in the house. As has been stated previously, an interpretation based on houses can be easily misleading.

The sensitive points are dubious in their value. In most cases they will not work out because they are calculated according to the Ascendant, and this is usually not precise, since the Ascendant and Midheaven move at an average rate of one degree in four minutes of time, and two degrees in eight minutes. These points, therefore, are only reliable if the chart has been rectified according to life events. But even here, it is evident that the half-sums of the stellar bodies are more important. Please refer to *Mensch im All.*

The bases for interpretation are treated in detail in *The Combination of Stellar Influences.*

Please note that the practical examples come from times in which things were different from the conditions of the present day.

Question: What will the coming year bring? Up to now, a prognostication was attempted by using the solar horoscope and the transits. More than twenty years ago I introduced the graphic forty-five degree ephemeris, and in the beginning, with little success. Today, many thousands in Germany alone are using this method, which in the meantime has excited interest in England, America, and Australia as well. This method enables you to obtain, within a few minutes' time, a survey on the year to come by writing the positions from the natal chart in the margin and then drawing straight lines through the graphic ephemeris form.

The forty-five degree ephemeris was developed from the ninety degree system, which was introduced in Germany more than fifty years ago. The great advantage of the ninety degree circle is that the aspects derived from the progressive division of the circle coincide in this diagram, i.e. conjunctions, squares and oppositions can be seen on the same spot, and it is not necessary first to check whether two stellar bodies form an angle of ninety degrees or 180 degrees. The semisquares and sesquiquadrates, angles of forty-five degrees and 135 degrees, are always opposite one another.

President Richard Nixon

We would like to take the example of the American President Richard Nixon (Illustration 10). In the inner 360 degree circle, the various stellar positions are simply marked on the degrees of the zodiacal signs. Around the outside, we have the ninety degree circle, and where the degrees from zero to thirty coincide with the signs Aries, Cancer, Libra, Capricorn, and the degrees from thirty to sixty with the signs Taurus, Leo, Scorpio, Aquarius, and finally, the degrees from sixty to ninety (zero degrees) with the signs Gemini, Virgo, Sagittarius, and Pisces (Illustration 11). Thus if Neptune at 24 Cancer 46 is to be transcribed, it will be entered in the outer ring at just before twenty-five degrees; Uranus at 2 Aquarius 42 would be placed just short of thirty-three degrees, and the Midheaven at 14 Gemini 41 would be marked at almost seventy-five degrees. Of course, some time is needed to get accustomed to this system, but the great merits of this method are more than worth the time expended in learning it.

If you want to observe several diagrams, for example of the members of your family, you need only line them up one after another, enabling you to spot the transits very quickly. If you know, for instance, that Pluto is at twenty-nine degrees Virgo, you only need to look up the eighty-ninth degree in each of the charts to know immediately that, in this case, Pluto is conjunct Mars and in other cases perhaps is conjunct other planets.

The forty-five degree ephemeris is more or less the same as the ninety degree circle, but in linear form, which only goes to forty-five degrees, since the semisquares and sesquiquadrates also have to be encompassed.

In the graphic ephemeris the months of the year can be found at the very top, and just below, the periods of ten days. On both sides are the divisions into degrees; on the right side this ranges from one to forty-five degrees, on the left side is forty-five degrees with the marking for each individual sign. If, for example, Mercury is located at zero degrees Capricorn, it then must accordingly be entered in the first section, where Capricorn is also to be found, i.e. at the very top where division into degrees begins. Jupiter must then come immediately after. But the Moon at twenty degrees Aquarius must be entered after the second version where Aquarius is also located, and so forth (Illustration 13).

In the transcription of the various positions from the ninety degree circle, the best procedure is to transcribe the positions from zero to

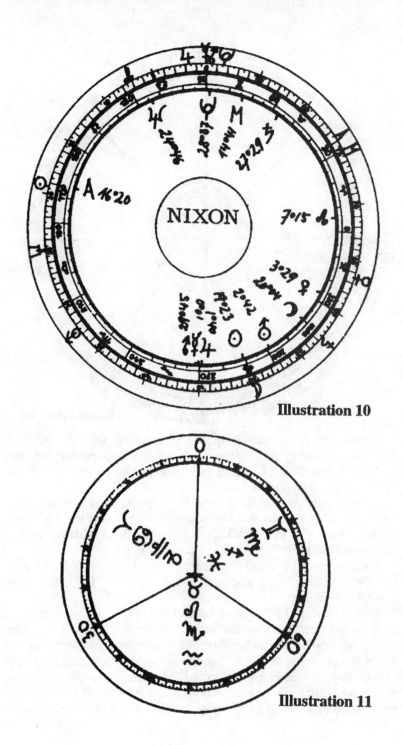

Illustration 10

Illustration 11

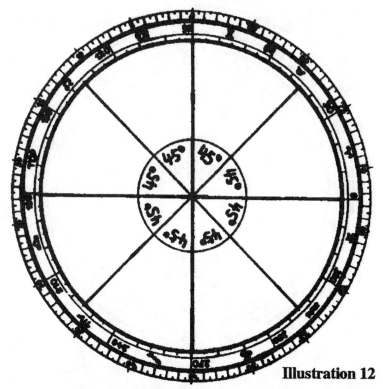

Illustration 12

forty-five degrees successively, thus eliminating any possibility of error. This is done by starting below at forty-five degrees and progressing through the circle of degrees until ninety degrees, and the various positions being thus entered.

By drawing horizontal lines across the page, points of intersection of the various stellar orbits will become evident. We note that the orbits of the slow moving planets take on a fairly flat form, whereas the fast moving planets move in an almost vertical plane.

In solar motion the small circles are marked by "N" for New Moon and "V" for Full Moon (German Voll = full). An "E" in the circle indicates an eclipse.

In each issue of the "Kosmischer Beobachter," the cosmo-political barometer is constructed on the basis of the graphic ephemerides. This cosmo-political barometer has provided the groundwork for around 150 political annual diagrams. All that has to be done is to check through each section for each month concerned and to transcribe the corresponding constellations. There is no other system in which it is possible to make a comparative check of many cosmograms at one time. Readers

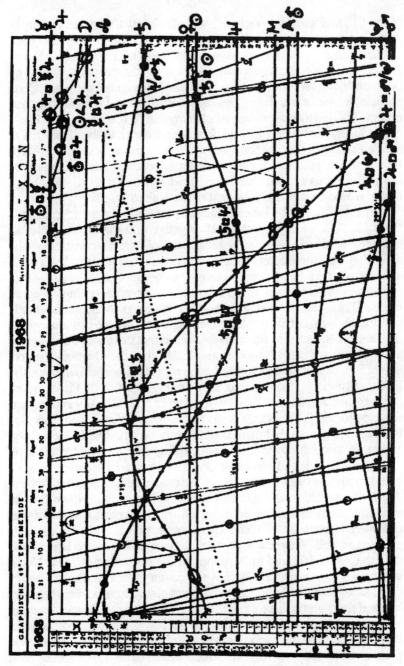

Illustration 13

95

of the "Kosmischer Beobachter" will also know that numerous prognostications have been made on this basis, and which have also been proven correct. For example, we will take the annual diagram for Nixon for the year 1968. As you know, the race for the presidency was run between Nixon and Humphrey in this year. Throughout the year, Nixon had less favorable and Humphrey considerably more favorable configurations. This led to the assumption of many that Nixon would most likely be the loser. However, I had made an exact check to the effect that at the beginning of November, just when the polling was due to start, favorable constellations for Nixon and unfavorable ones for Humphrey resulted. On this ground I could prognosticate that with all probability Nixon would be the next president of the United States.

In the marking of the various reaction points in the graphic ephemeris the back dots are to be valued as negative and the small circles as positive. In the case of several intersection points, I have written out the constellations, something I usually do not do since it generally is of no account whether these points relate to a conjunction, a square, or an opposition. Sextiles and trines cannot be encompassed in this ephemeris. This is not necessary because the object is to ascertain what is likely to happen. In this graphic ephemeris, then, we see that throughout the summer Saturn was square Neptune, so that there was little hope of any great gain of votes. It was only in October that the situation changed, where Jupiter and Uranus formed good aspects almost simultaneously. In succession, Jupiter entered into conjunctions with Pluto, Mars, Mercury and Jupiter, and then Uranus at first with Mercury and Jupiter. On November 9, as voting took place, Mars, Venus and Sun also transited Jupiter, so that there could hardly be any doubt of a victory, especially since the constellations for Humphrey were pretty negative.

There are other and numerous confirmations to be found in Nixon's annual diagram 1970, factors which the reader may remember. Around April 15, the astronauts returned from the Moon, and Nixon flew to welcome them in Hawaii on April 18. As we know, this flight was considered an event of some significance which added to Nixon's prestige as well. We see that in April, Jupiter first transited Uranus and then the Ascendant and Midheaven. At the beginning of May, Nixon sent troops to Cambodia to occupy the country. This aroused a wave of criticism against Nixon's tactics; the press placed him in a very negative light. Here, Saturn in progression transits Pluto and Mars; these are semisquares and sesquiquadrates. In addition, Uranus approaches a sesquiquadrate to the Moon, where an influence of long duration was present from May to July, at which time Nixon experienced great agitation and personal attacks. These attacks were strongest on May 26, when Saturn entered sesquiquadrate to Mercury. This should serve as

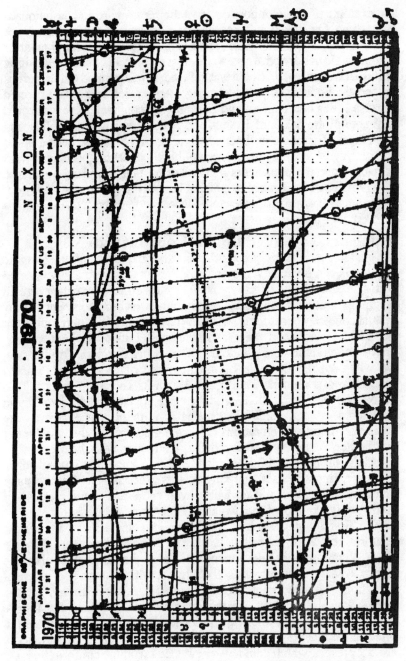

Illustration 14

one example of many of how decisive the semisquare and sesquiquadrate can be. On June 4, he experienced a defeat in that his strategy for the American South had failed, just as Saturn reentered sesquiquadrate to Jupiter. He underwent a renewed defeat on June 11, when a deposition of further troops to Cambodia was refused. It was pointed out in various prognostications that in midsummer greater tension was to be expected because at this point Saturn and Uranus were conjunct. Here we should take note of the orbits of Uranus and Saturn, which meet in July and September. The crisis in the Near East also arose in the period at the end of August to September. During this time, several airplanes were skyjacked and the passengers retained as hostages. And subsequently, the civil war in Jordan broke out, but Nixon was given no freedom of movement since he otherwise would have become involved in conflicts with Soviet Russia.

The Fairy Tale Wedding in Copenhagen

Greater sureness of prognostication on the basis of the graphic ephemeris can be achieved by comparing persons who are connected with one another by family or business ties in terms of their annual diagrams. This makes possible the simultaneous ascertainment of how mutual contact is constituted, whether the relationship is harmonious or filled with tension, and when favorable constellations for joint endeavors or unfavorable constellations will possibly develop. To illustrate, we will take the example of the marriage of the Crown Princess Margarete of Denmark with Prince Hendrik. The wedding is said to have run in perfect harmony, and the bride appeared "otherworldly in her happiness" at the side of her husband. With the princess there were some very good configurations due among others, for the axis Jupiter and Jupiter/Venus, Mars, coincided as a direction with the Moon.

Of the husband, Prince Hendrik, we only know the date of birth. However, in such cases there are factors ascertainable, despite there being no Ascendant and no Midheaven present. For the purpose of clarity, only extracts of the two annual diagrams are given here.

The first thing we see is that at various spots there are certain conformities. With the princess, there is a clustering of Sun, Moon's Node, Venus, Jupiter and Ascendant, and at the same place also, the Prince's Mars. It is obvious that this results in a strong physical attraction. The other points are less favorable, as for example when the female Pluto coincides with the male Uranus, or when the female Neptune is almost in line with the male Venus. The thing to keep in mind here is that the personal points, Ascendant, Midheaven, and Moon, are not present, which could also evidence favorable conformities.

The so-called "fairy tale wedding" took place in Copenhagen on

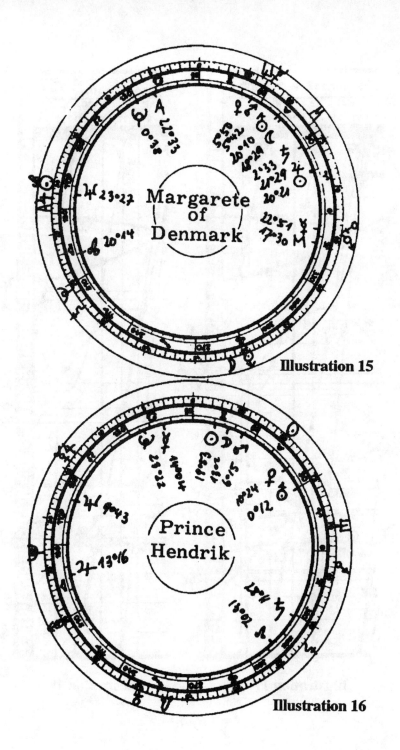

Illustration 15

Illustration 16

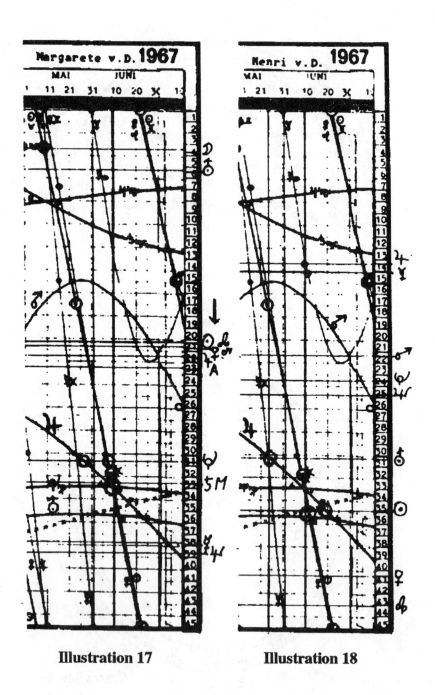

Illustration 17 **Illustration 18**

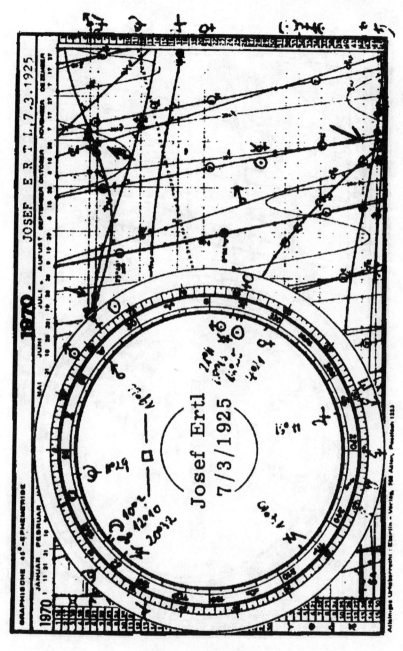

Illustration 19

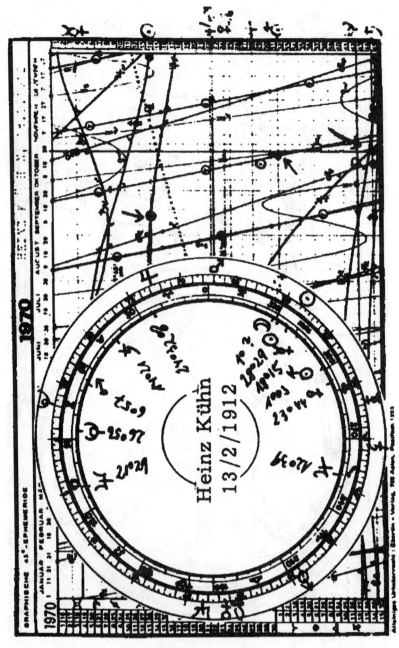

Illustration 20

June 10, 1967. As we can see, strong Jupiter transits are manifest in both cases: with the princess, Jupiter with Pluto over Midheaven, but also over Saturn, on the other hand, Sun and Venus transit the same point, so that in the case of the bride everything seems to center around the Midheaven.

With Prince Hendrik, however, Jupiter has just transited Uranus, and then, Jupiter, Venus and Sun are concentrated on the natal Sun of the partner.

It is not known whether the data have been calculated cosmically or not, but this example goes to how, in certain circumstances, the data of a wedding or the commencement of some special enterprise can be set or rather be made apparent for the partners. Of course, for a more exact investigation the natal chart itself will always be consulted and the aspects here, too, checked more closely. The structural pictures would also have to be considered.

Ministers and Illness

Daily events can also be observed with the aid of the annual diagrams. At the end of October, German newspapers reported that the Federal Minister Josef Ertl was seriously ill and on October 17 had to be taken to the hospital. On October 28, 1970, his condition was reported to be critical.

Looking at the annual diagram, we see that already in summer Saturn and Uranus transited the position lines of Mars and Neptune, which are square at the time of birth of the native on March 7, 1933; this constituted an axis of illness. The minister suffered a complete collapse due to overwork. A conjunction of Mars/Neptune indicates weakness and a paralysis (Neptune) of powers (Mars). This constellation was triggered by Mercury on October 10, and was again approached by Saturn as well as by Mars. This suffices to show that his condition is critical.

And yet, at the very bottom we see that Jupiter, after a few positive transits, transits Saturn jointly with Mars, which configuration Pluto after a time also joins.

This case was duplicated. Minister President Heinz Kühn, born February 18, 1912, suffered a heart attack on October 27 and had to be taken to the hospital immediately. We see from his annual diagram that in the summer Neptune was long in conjunction with the Sun, which corresponds to a heart disorder or a weak (Neptune) heart (Sun). On October 27 there are said to have been many upsets and disputes, as is evident in Sun = Uranus (upheaval). In addition, we see below, similar to the case of Ertl, that here Saturn is being "attacked" by Mars and Pluto.

The Saturn positions of the two politicians are in an aspect of 135 degrees. Thus in the forty-five degree system they are located on the same spot and triggered simultaneously. This shows how well suited annual diagrams are for the purpose of comparison. Calculations are not even required because of the easy comprehensibility of this method.

Our purpose here cannot be that of delving further into the use of the forty-five degree ephemeris. The scope of this book on transits can only allow a suggestion as to its application for a quick survey of the coming year.

You, the readers, may have seen from the examples presented that it is worthwhile trying out this method and setting up such annual diagrams for each member of your family, for the first at least, and making subsequent observations.

One point remains to be made in particular: It is by no means possible to grasp all occurrences using the transits alone; the directions must also be taken into consideration. In general, we can say that the directions are triggered by the transits. However, those aspects formed by the very slow moving planets such as Uranus, Neptune and Pluto are, in respect to their potency, equivalent to the directions.

The Frazier-Clay Fight

Frazier's winning was predicted.

The boxing match between Frazier and Clay was set for March 8, 1971. The whole world looked forward to this fight in the greatest of suspense. Although I have no particular interest in this sport, the many inquiries I received compelled me to examine the situation. I could only be told the birth dates, and not the hours of birth. After careful consideration I found Frazier's victory assured, and this was my answer to the inquiries.

Looking at the two cosmograms, we can immediately spot the constellations of decisive import for the fight and for its winning.

Clay, known for his brutality, has Mars square Pluto as the decisive constellation for his activity as a boxer. His chances lie especially in Sun sesquiquadrate Jupiter, his weaknesses in Neptune-135-Mars/Uranus.

With Frazier, the predominate and decisive constellation in respect to boxing is Mars conjunct Uranus-135-Sun. His chances lie especially in Pluto = Sun/Jupiter = Mercury/Uranus = Mercury/Mars. Frazier's weaknesses lie especially in Neptune = Sun/Saturn.

By transcribing the positions of the natal chart (horoscope) to the graphic forty-five degree ephemeris we can rapidly obtain a clear picture of the outcome of the fight on March 8, 1971.

In the case of Frazier, Saturn slowly approaches Neptune, but this constellation will not be due until the end of the month. Uranus passes

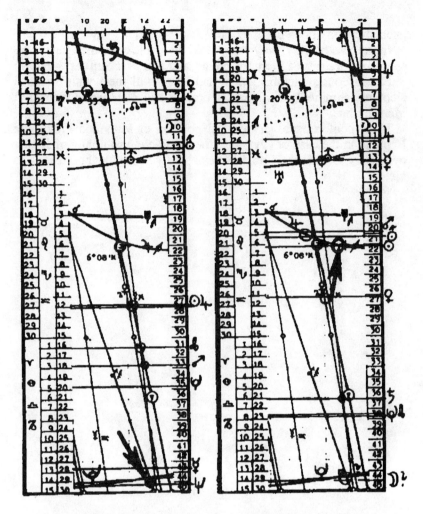

Illustration 21   **Illustration 22**

over Mercury (square) and approaches Jupiter.

The significant factor here is that Jupiter not only approaches the important constellation Mars = Uranus = Sun, but also apparently stands still, i.e. makes a station, lending Jupiter greater influence. Accordingly, Frazier could look forward to the fight with great confidence weeks ahead of time.

Mercury, Sun and Venus transit Saturn during this period, so that he also had to take some losses into account.

If the Moon be situated at about fourteen degrees Leo, Pluto and Mars would jointly transit the lunar position, which can mean an unusual intensification of power.

In the case of Clay, only very weak, favorable constellations can be seen in the transits of Mercury, Venus and Sun over Sun and Jupiter.

But in contrast to this, Mars and Pluto will meet with his natal Neptune, admittedly his weakest point, since Neptune is located at Mars/Uranus.

If we confront the very critical position of Mars and Pluto over Neptune in the case of Clay with the favorable positioning of Jupiter over Mars, Uranus and Sun, there can hardly be any doubt of Frazier's victory.